LEADERSHIP
in Congregations

LEADERSHIP
in Congregations

Richard Bass
Editor

Foreword by
Diana Butler Bass

THE
ALBAN
INSTITUTE
Herndon, Virginia
www.alban.org

The Alban Institute, 2121 Cooperative Way, Suite 100, Herndon, VA 20171

Library of Congress Cataloging-in-Publication Data

Leadership in congregations / edited by Richard Bass.
    p. cm. — (Harvesting the learnings)
 ISBN-13: 978-1-56699-334-0
 ISBN-10: 1-56699-334-2
 1. Pastoral theology—United States. 2. Christian leadership—United States. I. Bass, Richard (Richard W.)

 BV4011.3.L43 2006
 253—dc22

2006100542

11 10 09 08 07   VG   1 2 3 4 5

Contents

115152

Preface

"Leadership" has, of course, long been an interest of the Alban Institute. Our books are read by congregational leaders, our seminars attended by them, and they are the primary contacts for, and often the central focus of, the consulting work we do. In the past few years, however, we have stepped up our work on leadership, realizing that is through leaders that the ferment we hope for will reach the congregations we serve.

The signal moment of this new emphasis on leadership was the preparation and distribution in 2001 of the Alban Institute Special Report, "The Leadership Situation Facing American Congregations." In this report, Alban president James P. Wind and senior consultant Gil Rendle surveyed the "sea change" in American religion and examined the claims that congregational leadership was in crisis. They concluded that while evidence of both crisis and ferment were present, "the Alban Institute stands clearly on the side of ferment."

It was out of a desire to provide a permanent published record of that report that this book was born. But as we began to look through issues of our magazine, *Congregations,* it became clear that this was a topic on which we had long been working and continue to work. The articles collected here demonstrate the thoughtful and creative approaches to leadership taken by today's practitioners. I am grateful to all of their authors and to all of the other writers who have contributed to our ability to share the best writing from and for congregations.

We selected articles that we hoped would stimulate leaders with new perspectives on their work and roles. We honed in on the "pinch points" many leaders face when they have to learn how to lead in a new way: as the first woman pastor, as the pastor of a church that has learned not to depend on the staff, as the leader of a congregation in which consensus is not possible. Most of these writers go far beyond describing a situation, they tell us stories. And they live those stories. As Diana Butler Bass holds in her foreword, this is a key to effective leadership today.

We knew we were onto something when early in the preparation of this book we had an intern, a second-year seminarian, go through old issues of *Congregations* looking for articles that spoke to what she felt she needed to learn. By the end of the second day, she said that she had learned more in two days at the Alban Institute than she had in two years at her seminary—at least about congregational leadership. We hope that you too will find these writings instructive.

Richard Bass
Director of Publishing
The Alban Institute

Foreword: Living the Story

DIANA BUTLER BASS

For three years, I researched vital mainline Protestant congregations. Armed with a grant from the Lilly Endowment, I studied fifty churches to determine if there existed a common pattern of spiritual vibrancy and shared practices that strengthened communal life. Sifting through thousands of pages of data, my team pieced together both an overall pattern and leading practices in the study group, thus developing a picture of religious change, emerging vitality, and potential futures for mainline Protestantism.[1]

As a result of this project, many clergy groups have invited me to share my findings; I estimate that I have now addressed nearly 20,000 clergy and lay leaders across the United States (with a good number of Canadians in the mix). From place to place, people asked a variety of questions, engaging the research in productive ways. At *every* event, however, someone raised questions of leadership: "What did you observe about leadership? What kind of leadership nurtures the kind of vitality you found? What are the characteristics of the leaders in these congregations?" I quickly realized that in most cases people were asking me how they could lead their congregations into a richer life in God. And, sadly, they felt frustrated in their own attempts to be good leaders. The questions seemed to come from their own spiritual hunger, a nagging sense of failure as congregational leaders, or anxiety about their leadership performance.

My research team did not directly study leadership in vital congregations—we hoped to make that the topic of a later grant. Early on, I actually tried to avoid questions of leadership, feeling vaguely inadequate to address the topic and having no specific data to share. I worry that leadership is difficult to discuss and prone to "magic bullet" solutions of quick-fix gurus. The questions kept coming, however, and although I had no hard data, I realized that I had observed good leadership in the participating congregations. In *The Practicing Congregation*, the first book published about the project, I identified an emerging style of "narrative leadership" for congregational renewal.[2]

Narrative leadership is a deceptively simple principle: *know your story and live it.* Some people know stories and tell them well but live without intentional connection to those stories; others simply experience quotidian life with no reflection on larger stories of meaning. In vital mainline churches, leaders knew their stories and lived them—thus turning the power of narrative into a source of and resource for change.

While *The Practicing Congregation* was primarily theoretical, this essay develops narrative leadership by discerning four pathways of practice in the study churches. These pathways serve as entry points for those unfamiliar with this vision of leadership and signposts to keep current practitioners moving ahead. They include: (1) story shapes leadership; (2) leaders shape stories; (3) narrative leadership is character and context driven; and (4) leadership is based in charisma, not celebrity.

Pathway 1: Story Shapes Leadership

The stories about American religion shape our expectations of leadership. For example, "the Titanic" storyline dominates how we talk about mainline Protestantism. We think of mainline Protestant denominations as a doomed ocean liner, the ship has hit an iceberg (political conflict, numerical decline, or some other crisis) and is sinking. Denominational officials are accused of "rearranging deck chairs on the Titanic." People regularly remark, "We're going down," or "We can't turn this ship around." Once, I heard an Episcopalian refer to her priest as "the chaplain on the Titanic."

If we think of churches as the Titanic, that has serious implications for leadership—our bishops, conference ministers, pastors, and priests are required to rescue us. Throw people in lifeboats. Fix the big hole in the ship. Save whoever—and whatever—can be saved. From this perspective, leadership is an emergency rescue operation, heroic but hopeless. We all know the end of the story. The ship will sink. The best our leaders can do is to save a few—and maybe themselves. No wonder so many pastors are anxious and depressed. Who wants to lead in this scenario?

But what if the Titanic is not the story? A better story—and perhaps more accurate in current circumstances—may be that of the Mayflower. In this story, a boat of pilgrims finds itself in uncharted seas, blown off course by a storm and heading to an unnamed country. Like the Titanic story, there is a sense of urgency, confusion, and fear. But the ship is intact as it sails off course from the intended colony of Virginia. Here, leaders are not trying to patch the hull or load lifeboats. They are not praying for a miracle. Instead, they look for land. They keep calm while providing focus, vision, and direction, while they navigate the choppy—if unfamiliar—seas of the north Atlantic. Once they do reach land, leaders envision a way to structure the new community and take part in building a new life.

In the Titanic story, leaders lead while the ship is sinking. In the Mayflower story, leadership stabilizes a pilgrim community in choppy seas as they head for an unknown world. Leadership in a crisis? Or leadership as an adventure? How a leader leads and the expectations a community has about leadership depends on the stories we tell ourselves.

Pathway 2: Leaders Shape Stories

Closely related to this is the capacity of leaders to shape stories. These days, one of the primary capacities of good leadership is to enable people to understand change, interpret chaos, and make sense of a seemingly meaningless world. There are a variety of ways for leaders to make meaning—some religions practice this sort of leadership through creedal conformity, dictates, demands, or intellectual certainty. But another route to meaning-making is through storytelling.

Throughout my research on vital mainline churches, both clergy and congregational leaders were storytellers. They knew their own faith stories, they knew the stories of their congregations, they knew their tradition's stories, and they knew the larger Christian and biblical stories. They exhibited ease and comfort in sharing these stories and invited others into a variety of stories in natural and authentic ways. In the process, they opened paths for other people to learn and tell stories of faith. And they ably moved between personal, congregational, and biblical stories to create worlds of spiritual and theological meaning. They intuited the power of story to rearrange people's lives—using story in much the same way Jesus did—and to open windows to spiritual realities and alternative paths that sometimes escape life's more mundane interpretations.

And, of course, storytelling leaders have the ability to change the story in which they exercise leadership! Scripts can be rewritten. A good leader will be able to move a congregation away from deadening and fear-filled stories, like that of the Titanic, toward life-giving possibilities of faithful adventure.

Pathway 3: Leadership Is Character and Context Driven

Every pastoral leader I met—and every lay leader I interviewed—acted as a uniquely formed "character" in his or her story. Each person had a specific faith journey, each particular gifts for leadership, each a distinctive vision of God's reign, and each a set of practices that shaped ministry. In no circumstance did any person resemble a clone of another—they allowed their personhood to shape their leadership practices. They understood that leadership emerged from the crucible of personal health and healthy relationships—it was not guaranteed on the basis of a role they held or an external authority structure. The more individuals leaned into their own strengths, the more they trusted who God made them to be, the more richly they discovered their own abilities as leaders.

Although they demonstrated no single set of characteristics, there were some leadership commonalities across the study. They did not depend on external definitions of leadership, but they were familiar with a variety of leadership theories and tools. Nearly all the clergy had read Ron Heifetz's book *Leadership Without Easy Answers* and practiced adaptive leadership in concert with appropriate use of technical skills.[3] They were good pastors and preachers; they knew their strengths and weaknesses; they exercised humor and humility. And they realized their own ministry was strengthened in relation to the whole of the congregation (this was true for lay leaders as well).

Thus, uniqueness existed within the context of community. Good character-driven leadership did not rise above or control the congregation on the basis of personality or charisma. Instead, religious leadership functioned best in a connected network of relationships; characters worked in concert with each other deepening and developing the larger plotlines of the congregation. In developing connection, there needed to be some sort of "match" or "fit," some sort of almost indefinable meshing, between the personhood of the leader and the congregation context. In the language of story, characters need to live reflexively with the setting.

Many of the pastors in my project had learned this through experience. A good number of them had struggled in earlier placements or calls—they never connected because the settings were wrong for their own character. But when the clergy person found his or her way to the "right" congregation, then their own practice of leadership soared. Excellent pastoral leadership is, indeed, individual and unique, but it is not separate or singular; it is deeply embedded in the context of community. And it must be developed there in healthy, emotionally mature, and spiritually wise ways.

Pathway 4: Leadership Is Based in Charisma, not Celebrity

When quizzed about the pastors in my project, other clergy frequently ask if these leaders were particularly charismatic and if congregational renewal depended upon a strong personality. Most of the time, this question was posed in a critical manner—as if there is something inappropriate or dangerous about charismatic leadership. Indeed, many of the clergy who participated in the study were interesting and talented people, with varying levels of personal charisma. Their charisma was distinct from religious celebrity. Rather, charisma—giftedness in the biblical sense—emerged from integrity through practicing what they preached.

Many congregants praised their clergy (or other spiritual leaders in their churches) as "real" or "authentic." They related a number of characteristics with authenticity, including the ability to relate to a wide

variety of people, being open, accessible, funny, and "very human."
However, along with such down-to-earth qualities, congregants further extolled spiritual leaders who embodied their theological beliefs
through identifiable Christian practices. Congregations wanted ministers who practiced hospitality, stayed centered in prayer, ordered their
economic lives through stewardship and generosity, and testified to
God's transforming grace in their own experience. Thus, a mixture of
personable "just like us" qualities and the ability to model practical
spirituality seemed optimal for leaders.

Clergy and other spiritual leaders may find this difficult, but I
thought these expectations surprisingly humane. Leaders need to be
serious faith practitioners, people who "walk the talk" and live out the
things they hope will change the lives of others. However, the congregations in my project did not want a pastor's devotion to separate the
minister and people; they did not appear to want super-saints as leaders. They wanted spiritually mature, very human leaders—the same
balance they hoped to achieve in their own lives.

Leaders in the study cultivated a life of practice. But they knew
that not every person is called to every Christian practice—some people
are more gifted or skilled at certain ones. Thus, the ministers prayed,
but they recognized that others might be more mature in the practice
of prayer and willingly became learners in relation to able practitioners. They knew when to lead in practice, and they equally knew when
to learn from the wisdom of other people in the congregation. Religious leaders need to practice what they preach, but they need not be
perfect in their practice. Practicing what one preaches does not imply
perfection. Rather, it means creating a certain level of congruence between proclaiming faith and demonstrating it in one's life.

One of the most dramatic cultural shifts of the last thirty
years is in the role storytelling plays in our lives; story has become a
primary path to meaning-making. Sociologist Anthony Giddens claims
that our identity is found "in the on-going story about the self" and
further asserts that "each of us not only 'has' but *lives* a biography."[4]
Moral philosopher Charles Taylor says that we understand life as an
"unfolding story" in which "we grasp our lives as narrative."[5] Put simply, we become ourselves as we tell our stories. We cannot know our-

selves apart from our stories—stories in which we are both author and actor. When these philosophical principles are expanded beyond the individual to congregation, the power of narrative leadership is easily grasped and naturally enacted.[6] To lead is to create story and to act in concert with the tale.

Notes

1. For more on the this project and its findings, see Diana Butler Bass, *The Practicing Congregation: Imagining a New Old Church* (Herndon, VA: Alban Institute, 2004); Diana Butler Bass and Joseph Stewart-Sicking, *From Nomads to Pilgrims: Stories from Practicing Congregations* (Herndon, VA: Alban Institute, 2006); and Diana Butler Bass, *Christianity for the Rest of Us: How the Neighborhood Church is Transforming the Faith* (San Francisco: HarperSanFrancisco, 2006). See also www.dianabutlerbass.com and www.practicingcongregations.org.
2. Bass, *The Practicing Congregation*, 91–102.
3. Ronald A. Heifetz, *Leadership without Easy Answers* (Cambridge, MA: The Belknap Press of Harvard University, 1994).
4. Anthony Giddens, *Modernity and Self-Identity* (Stanford, CA: Stanford University Press, 1991), 54 (punctuation and italics in the original).
5. Charles Taylor, *Sources of the Self* (Cambridge, MA: Harvard University Press, 1989), 47.
6. For the transformative power of story in congregations, see Lillian Daniel, *Tell It Like It Is: Reclaiming the Practice of Testimony* (Herndon, VA: Alban Institute, 2006).

The Leadership Situation Facing American Congregations: An Alban Institute Special Report

JAMES P. WIND AND GIL RENDLE

Introduction

If someone were to write an article for one of our major newspapers or newsmagazines about the leadership situation facing American congregations and their leaders, what would the headline be? Preliminary research at the Alban Institute suggests "A Sea Change in American Religion: American Congregational Leaders Face Great Ferment and Turmoil." In our conversations with religious leaders around the country, we have participated in a strong debate as to which word or phrase best describes our reality. Some of these leaders focus on turmoil, saying that we are in a time of great crisis and that American religion still has not faced up to the depths of its predicament despite mountains of statistics about decline and countless stories of institutional pain. Others say that we have been blinded by all the turmoil and crisis talk and have missed the ferment, growth, and new vitality emerging in many places in American religious life.

In our own conversations, we have been deeply pulled by both sides of this argument. In fact, we find ourselves coming to the seemingly paradoxical conclusion that both realities—turmoil and ferment, crisis and opportunity—constitute the depth of the sea change that we are now experiencing. Indeed, it is the paradoxical character of this

Originally published as an Alban Institute Special Report in September 2001 with the generous support of Lilly Endowment Inc. and The Henry Luce Foundation, Inc.

1

period of great transition in American religion—one filled with emergent vitality on the one hand and systemic dysfunction on the other—that makes ours such a complex time. Keeping both sides of the reality in responsible tension as we describe the situation is one of the greatest challenges when discussing the need for renewed leadership. We believe that to stand on the side of ferment includes acknowledging and even embracing the reports of crisis, for these are the signs of a system grappling with deep issues—a system that is fundamentally healthy enough to put up a fight.

The Field of Inquiry

In traditional Alban Institute fashion, we began our efforts to probe more deeply into this complex leadership situation by talking to practitioners and experts who have considerable wisdom about what is happening in congregations and in the larger context of American religion. We began with interviews of a select group of religious leaders and experts who represent the worlds of congregational ministry, judicatory administration, denominational research, theological education, philanthropy, and consulting.[1] As our inquiry broadened, we tested the results of our initial research with numerous groups of religious leaders in a variety of educational and public settings. We read reports and available research and searched broadly for more. We then tested our learnings against our own practice and experience with congregations across North America and across many different faith traditions.

Research Base

As we searched for data and spoke with practitioners and experts, we quickly realized that there is *no coordinated, systematic research base* from which to draw specific conclusions about the leadership situation in American religion. We found that those whose careers are devoted to funding and conducting research on American religion stressed this fact most. Instead of a solid research base, these people pointed us to a variety of isolated reports that they felt revealed certain key realities. So there are many pieces of evidence, but they are of uneven quality and do not fully cover the area of inquiry. The implication is clear: *We lack thorough, high-quality, empirically based research on this important topic.* This was especially true as we looked for studies or research within ethnic minority congregational and denominational systems or within the evangelical church tradition.

As we continue to search for this information, we find that in all of these areas, including the mainline Protestant traditions, no single study or group of studies pulls together the various elements of our current situation and allows for a coherent set of generalizations and impressions. This is a situation we plan to address in our continuing work on congregational leadership. Meanwhile, we are left with a set of sightings and soundings from various places in the American religious ecology. We intend for these observations to be just the beginning of an important conversation, and we hope that it will continue among all who care for our congregations.

Laying the Groundwork

It is interesting that the turmoil and crisis side of the story was much more prominent in the interviews and discussions we had than the conversation about ferment. Clearly, there are major immediate challenges facing American congregations and their leaders. As the rest of this report will show, we know much more about the crises that drive us than we do of the fuller power of the sea change. For this reason, Part 1 of this report describes these crises as reflected in a scattering of available reports on this dominant interpretation of our current setting. Yet our discussions with others also lifted up the lesser-known reality of the ferment in our sea change and encouraged us not to be so fixated on the crisis at hand that we miss the larger reality. Part 2 of this report will turn to this part of our discovery.

Part 1: Rehearsing the Crisis

The first part of the story is the prevailing sense of crisis about established religious institutions. A large scholarly literature exists about certain aspects of this crisis, such as membership decline in mainline denominations. But other parts of the crisis are not as widely known and we want to point to three—shortage of clergy, quality of clergy, and retention of women in ministry—that can tell us a great deal about the larger crisis.

It is not surprising that these indicators are related to the current clergy leadership system in American religion. The state of clergy recruitment, preparation, and deployment stand as bellwether indicators for many religious leaders. This is consistent with Alban Institute experience, which recognizes that while there are multiple factors influencing the vitality of congregations and congregational systems, clergy leadership is a central point of attention and diagnosis. Alban's experience of working with congregations underlines the reality that congregations cannot rise above their leadership, that faith communities cannot develop large visions without visionary leaders.

Many in the American religious ecology who are more sensitive to and aware of the crisis side of the current sea change have produced numerous studies that probe various parts of the crisis more closely. Since these allow us to take deeper soundings, we will briefly summarize important insights from several such studies in the pages that follow.

Indicator 1: Shortage of Clergy

A key finding in our interviews was that most of the major Christian and Jewish denominations are experiencing or soon will face a shortage of clergy to meet current congregational demands. (Not all denominations are presently experiencing a shortage; the Unitarian Universalist Association, for example, reports a surplus.) In some cases, like Roman Catholicism, this shortage has been long recognized. Researchers from within the Roman Catholic Church provide ample evidence. R. Scott Appleby, from the University of Notre Dame, offers a telling summary footnote that describes the leadership sea change that has occurred in his church body during the past 40 years:

> In 1960 United States Catholicism boasted the low-cost, labor-intensive dedication of 52,689 priests and 164,922 nuns. More than 30,000 young men filled diocesan and religious-order seminaries. . . . Since 1960 the Catholic population has grown from 40 to approximately 55 million, but the number of priests (45,000 in 1994) and women religious (90,000) has declined as a result of resignations, retirements,

and thinning ranks of recruits. By 1994 the number of seminarians at all levels of study had dropped to about 5,100, hardly enough to replace the wave of retirements on the near horizon, much less to keep up with the increasing size of the laity.[2]

What does this mean for the average Catholic parish? In May 2000, researchers Jim Castelli and the Rev. Eugene Hemrick released results of the *National Catholic Parish Survey*, which concluded that:

- The average parish, which has 2,831 members and 5.1 ministers, is served by 1.8 ordained priests.
- 19 percent of those priests are either retired or living in residence in the parish but serving in another role elsewhere.

Moreover, since 1982:

- The number of priests serving the average parish has fallen by 28 percent.
- The number of religious serving the average parish has fallen by 33 percent.
- The number of deacons serving the average parish has fallen by 33 percent.
- The number of lay ministers serving the average parish has grown by 54 percent.[3]

These momentous changes in American Catholicism do not have exact parallels in other parts of the American religious world. Interestingly, just a few years ago many Protestant denominations expressed worry about clergy oversupply. But our informants indicate that many other denominations now find themselves sharing this concern over clergy shortages with the largest religious community in America. In 1997 the Rev. Rolf Memming, in his study of the trends in ordination and clergy careers for Division of Ordained Ministry of the United Methodist Church, reported a six-year slump in the number of ordinations of clergy in that denomination beginning in 1989.[4] This slump produced a downward trajectory that has left some wondering if there will be enough United Methodist clergy to serve the church in coming years.

Similarly, the Evangelical Lutheran Church in America (ELCA) reports in *Ministry Needs and Resources in the 21st Century* that "the number of pastors in the ELCA has declined slowly over the past decade so that some synods now experience a near critical shortage." A key part of the ELCA story is "an increase in the number of smaller congregations with very limited financial resources." More precisely, the report stated:

- From 1988 to 1998, the number of smaller congregations with average worship attendance of 50 or fewer increased from 2,058 to 2,329 (21.4 percent).
- In 1998, 4,000 (36.8 percent) congregations reported 75 worshipers or fewer.
- 5,453 (50 percent) congregations reported 100 or fewer worshipers in 1998.[5]

The report goes on to state that these small congregations are finding it increasingly difficult to recruit and retain ordained clergy, that pastoral vacancies are increasing and lasting longer, that ministerial supply is not keeping up with demand (the February 2000 candidate assignment process for new seminary graduates had 211 available candidates for 445 positions) and that "the number of clergy leaving ordained ministry through on-leave-from-call, resignation, removal and retirement" was putting additional pressure on the clergy deployment system.

According to the recent National Congregations Study, one of the richest and most comprehensive contemporary studies of American congregations, this ELCA picture is remarkably similar to a larger pattern within the reality of congregations in American life. The survey reports that the American religious experience still is heavily skewed toward small congregations in which the median worship attendance is 75 persons.[6] This would suggest that the ELCA pattern of small congregations' difficulties in recruiting and retaining ordained clergy is, or may be soon, more widespread.

The Presbyterian Church (U.S.A.) has a similar story. Kurtis C. Hess, a professor at Union Theological Seminary-Presbyterian School for Christian Education in Richmond, Virginia, reports that the number of church professionals available for church positions in his denomination is decreasing fairly rapidly. The decline has several dimensions:

- A smaller number of people entering congregational ministry. Presbyterian placement officers reported in 1999 that "only

50-60 percent of our [Presbyterian] students are going into parish ministry." In marked contrast to 15 years previously when the norm was between 80 percent and 90 percent, the "national offices in Louisville verified that only 50 percent of the 1998 graduates went into parish ministry."

- Retirement of clergy. Hess's report states: "The ranks of retired clergy are increasing rapidly. 8,800 out of 10,300 will have retired by 2025; 1/3 of those currently in seminary will retire by that date."
- Shorter clergy-career tenures. The denomination's Board of Pensions found that "pastors remain in the parish for an average of only 17 years." Further, Hess states that the PCUSA is "approaching the sad fact that almost 20 percent of those who enter parish ministry will leave the pastorate within 5 years of ordination." All of this adds up to an ominous bottom line. From 1993 to 1998, the denomination lost an average of 111 clergy per year. In 1998, 33 percent of PCUSA congregations did not have an installed pastor. If present trends continue, the supply of clergy serving congregations in this denomination will have declined from 8,739 in 1993 to 5,500 in 2025.[7]

From a supply perspective, the graying of the ministerium that has been noted for some time seems to be an important prevailing trend. This trend carries with it these three implications:

1. We will face many retirements.
2. The people who choose to follow the retirees will often have shorter pastoral careers due to later age of entry in the profession.
3. More laypeople will be claiming places in congregational leadership.

This graying of the ministerium and the growing clergy shortage is matched by the dearth of young clergy leaders available in many of our denominations. Recently an issue of the Alban Institute magazine, *Congregations,* focused on the lack of young clergy and received a surprising response from concerned and alarmed readers. Much of the response focused on the reporting of denominational statistics that showed alarming drops in the number of clergy age 35 and younger. Comparing statistics from the mid-1970s to the present moment, there were notable decreases in the percentage of clergy in the 35 and younger category—from 24 percent in 1975 to 7 percent in 1999 for the Presbyterian Church (U.S.A.), from 19 percent in 1974 to 4 percent in 2000 for the Episcopal Church, and from 18 percent in 1980 to 8 percent in 2000 for the Lutheran Church–Missouri Synod.[8]

Whatever the long-term effects of these changes may be—and they are still unknowable—it is clear that many of the assumptions about clergy leadership in congregations require reexamination. Not so long ago, some denominations urged candidates for the ministry to get "real world" experience before ordination; today, they decry the paucity of young clergy. The role of lay professionals in the church is also changing, with many moving from support functions to leadership positions that would have previously been filled by clergy.

Indicator 2: Quality of Pastoral Leadership

Recently a group of presbytery leaders from around the country concluded that "a crisis in pastoral leadership is sweeping across the Presbyterian Church (U.S.A.)." "This crisis is not only a shortage of women and men to fill pastoral positions in congregations; it is also a decline in the quality of those whom the church is calling to the office of minister of the Word and Sacrament."[9] This concern with clergy quality is widespread across denominations and faith traditions.

For example, American Judaism also is responding to a similar sense of crisis in rabbinic leadership. According to the recent report of the Reconstructionist Commission on the Role of the Rabbi, the clergy shortage is related to discomfort with the role of ordained leadership within the congregation. "Rabbis and rabbinical students increasingly indicate a reluctance to serve in congregational settings. They cite several common concerns: that the job is simply unmanageable; that boundaries between personal and professional time cannot be established; that the variety of roles they must fill creates unreasonable expectations and confusing standards of evaluation; that an absence of efficient and effective models of decision making, communication and leadership hinders their work."[10] Clearly the conversation about the quality or competence of leadership oscillates between an exploration of the quality of the person, along with his or her preparation for the role of leader, and the lack of clarity or reasonableness of the role of leader itself.

Related to the shortage of clergy noted previously, this concern over the competence of people who are entering ministry was expressed by our informants in several ways. Some were worried that new clergy simply do not have the talents, skills, and knowledge they need to become effective leaders. This deficit was at times attributed to certain lacks in the talent pool; at other times it was laid at the door of the seminaries. This concern about the quality of ministerial candidates has been recurrent since the nineteenth century. Others were worried that seminary students often enter denominations in which they have little experience. They expressed concern that students came to seminaries with low levels of religious literacy and with high personal and therapeutic needs. Still others noted that a large number of seminarians are not interested in seeking congregational leadership positions.

Recent statistics from the Association of Theological Schools (ATS) helped sharpen this reading about the supply pipeline:

- Of the 3,009 students graduating from 90 seminaries in 1999, 60 percent were in the M.Div. track.
- An important part of this supply portrait has to do with gender: males composed 65 percent of these graduates, females 35 percent. (Remember that these figures include Catholic seminaries—mainline Protestant denominations have seen a more rapid influx of women in the past 40 years than is indicated by these numbers.)
- Of those in the professional track for ordained parish ministry, 61 percent of male graduates and 54 percent of female graduates were expecting to serve as full-time parish clergy.
- When asked about their plans five years down the road, only 53 percent of male M.Div. graduates and 48 percent of females expected to still be in parish ministry.
- More than 40 percent of M.Div. students were age 40 or older.

The ATS survey also tells us that the increasing racial and ethnic diversity of students preparing at our seminaries does not keep pace with the increasing diversity of our population as a whole.

As to assessments of competence, the ATS has tracked GRE verbal scores. From 1981 to 1987, prospective women M.Div. students consistently scored above the mean for all examinees (in one year just barely). Male students consistently scored below the mean. The range of scores for women was from 500 to 520, for men 485 to 495.[11]

Individual denominations have their own ways of tracking declining quality. For the Presbyterian Church (U.S.A.), this issue is addressed in the *Presbyterian Outlook* article on the crisis in pastoral leadership cited at the beginning of this section. The writers of this article expressed concern about the "unacceptable failure rates on standard ordination exams, especially in biblical exegesis (31 percent in February 1999 and 39 percent in September 1999), theological competence (40 percent and 31 percent in 1999) and church polity (36 percent and 38 percent in 1999)." They noted with concern that presbyteries could not obtain "standard ordination pass-fail rates of each Presbyterian theological institution" and the "temptation of presbyteries to circumvent ordination requirements through the use of 'extraordinary' clauses and oral exams." When looking at the pool of ministerial candidates they found "certain attitudes and behaviors of some recent seminary graduates which undermined or impeded pastoral ministry: inability to analyze and understand congregations as systems, poor interpersonal skills, poor leadership skills, lack of maturity, failure to keep ethical norms and boundaries, and failure to take responsibility for self, including personal health." It was time, they concluded, for the denomination to raise its standard and recruit the "brightest and best." [12]

The United Methodist Church, in reviewing its own trends of decreasing numbers of ordinands, questioned the quality of the people who responded to the call of ministry seeking ordination. Quoting Perkins School of Theology professor Schubert Ogden, Rolf Memming's report observed that "fewer and fewer undergraduate students who graduated at the top of their classes are coming to theological classes. They are going on to other professions and careers." The study also cited evidence of reluctance among some United Methodist clergy to encourage others to enter ministry, suggesting a breakdown of both formal and informal channels of calling "the brightest and best" to leadership.[13]

A recent study conducted by the Auburn Center for the Study of Theological Education further refines our picture of the supply side of the congregational leadership story. Auburn's careful survey of seminary students looked across the spectrum of American Theological Schools at students beginning seminary education in 1998.[14] The study indicates that a major shift is taking place in the supply pool for American clergy. A different kind of student is entering the seminary today, bringing different kinds of resources to the leadership pool. "Students entering theological schools today are—as so many have observed—older than students are reported to have been in the past. On average they are much older than students entering medical and law schools, which have collected recent data describing their students. Women, who were a tiny percentage of students in the early 1970s, now make up about one-third of the entering student body, and as much as one-half in some religious sectors. Racial and ethnic representation is comparable to that in other professional schools, but African-Americans and Hispanics are significantly underrepresented compared with their presence in the general population."

The report moves beyond demographic realities and probes the background of these students. "Much of the evidence suggests that most of today's students come to theological school from a congregation rather than a campus. A majority of students make their decisions about theological study and ministry relatively late, after college graduation, and they do not major in subjects in the humanities that in the past were recommended as relevant pre-seminary study." There seemed to be little evidence that the old "feeder system" of church-related colleges was a significant factor in recruiting these students.

What about the quality of these students? "Theological schools are not highly selective (data from other sources show that half accept 87 percent or more of those who apply). A majority of students apply to only one school. Only a handful say that they were not accepted by their first choice of seminary." The report noted that this was a very different pattern from other professions like law and medicine, which were much more selective and competitive.

Finally, the report reminds us that not all of these students intend to serve in congregational leadership roles. "Though 80 percent say that their goal is a 'religious' profession or occupation, fewer (60 percent) plan to be ordained, and ministry in a congregation or parish is the goal of less than one-third of students."

Looking at more seasoned and experienced clergy, a study conducted by researchers Alan C. Klaas and Cheryl D. Klaas paints a very dismal picture of one denomination's situation. The Lutheran Church–Missouri Synod (LCMS), which commissioned the study, is one of the more conservative Lutheran Church bodies in America and is not normally lumped together with mainline denominations. Thus it is surprising to read about a malaise and decline of troubling proportions. Beginning with the fact that the denomination had lost 1,305 clergy between 1988 and 1997, the study piles up a set of troubling statistics. The Synod's Council of Presidents reports that 15 percent of its congregational leadership positions are vacant and that unless trends change drastically, 24 percent of its congregations will not have a pastor in 2007. Right now the church body expects the shortage to increase even more dramatically through 2017.

The Klaases set out to understand the reason for the shortage. In an amazingly thorough system-wide survey and interview project the researchers talked to clergy, seminary faculty, denominational executives, clergy family members, seminarians, their spouses, and students in the denomination's college and high schools (what used to be the feeder system for its seminaries). They discovered a sick denominational system. They assert that "a harsh and intolerant spirit is poisoning the infrastructure of the LCMS." They found that 30 percent of the clergy truly loved their work and served as effective role models for others who might one day enter the ministry. Another 30 percent were deeply ambivalent about their ministry. These clergy noted positive aspects of ministry but then immediately turned to systemic issues that led to expressions of "modest levels of despair—which they are quick to pull back into check and repress."

Another 20 percent are in what the Klaases term "advanced stages of burnout." That means that over 1,000 clergy are "in depression and despair, either unaware of or not trusting 'official' channels of help." The remaining 20 percent are "well on their way to burnout."[15]

As an overall indicator the researchers pointed to the response they received to what they felt was a simple and neutrally worded question, "What is it like being a parish pastor these days?" Two-thirds of the responses were negative and these were given with denominational officials and other clergy sitting at the interview table with them. The Klaases conclude their report with a list of problems they have identified that are factors in explaining why the Synod faces its clergy shortage. They include:

1. people beating on each other;
2. mismatch of pastors and congregations;
3. the difficulty getting help to pastors;
4. poor support for clergy wives and children (the Synod does not ordain women);
5. low clergy income;
6. grossly unreasonable expectations of pastors;
7. fighting and sick congregations; and
8. congregations where a few members dominated the vast majority.

The Klaases also list a series of problems related to the recruitment of new ministers.[16]

To risk a vast understatement, this is a very troubling portrait of an American denomination at the turn of the century. To be sure, there are specific factors in this story peculiar to this one denomination's history (the deep and ongoing struggle in the church body to maintain sound doctrine and practice based on inerrant Scriptures) that others do not share. And the researchers' agenda and methods may have something to do with the outcomes. But it is interesting to us that our informants, none of whom were in this denomination, knew of this study and felt that some of what is described here—especially the separation of clergy into positive, ambivalent, and deeply troubled cohorts—rang true in other parts of the American religious environment.

The Lutheran Church–Missouri Synod is not the only place where warning signs about clergy morale and health surface. A recent mailing from PastorCare: The National Clergy Support Network, a group devoted to helping "needy pastors," reported on findings from a 1991 survey of 1,000 U.S. pastors conducted by the Fuller Institute of Church Growth. Among the troubling findings:

- 80 percent of pastors believe their pastoral ministry has negatively affected their families.
- 75 percent reported a significant stress-related crisis at least once in their ministry.
- 50 percent felt unable to meet the demands of the job.
- 90 percent felt inadequately trained to cope with ministry demands.
- 70 percent have a lower self-image than when they began their professions.
- 50 percent had considered leaving the ministry within the three months prior to completing the survey.[17]

Our own experience at the Alban Institute, while it cannot confirm or refute these statistics, gives additional evidence of the pressures on clergy. Both our consultation and educational work on the one hand, and the inquiries we receive for information about resources to help clergy deal with "burnout" and to help create centers that can deal with clergy health issues on the other, suggest that many clergy are clearly struggling. The fact that many of the denominations have launched major clergy wellness initiatives provides further evidence that there is great pain in the clergy system.

When raising the question of competency of clergy leaders, it is necessary to look at the systems in which those leaders are placed for support, accountability, and development. While the full research base is unavailable to describe our current setting, once more there are examples of individual studies that can deepen our view. In this case we turn to the Project on the Spiritual Development Needs of Mid-Career Clergy. This report, done under the auspices of the Toronto School of Theology, provides another angle of vision on the denominational systems in which clergy live. In this report William Lord and John C. Bryan deliberately set out to survey and interview clergy who "were not currently in crisis mode" about both their sense of adequacy in meeting the spiritual needs of their church members and about their personal spiritual needs. They worked with a small sample (80 surveyed and 45 interviewed) of American and Canadian Protestant clergy who were nominated by judicatory leaders because they met the criteria of being mid-career (at least 15 years in ministry and at least 10 more years of active ministry anticipated), effective, and successful.

The researchers discovered that significant percentages of these clergy "did not feel adequately prepared to help their parishioners" when approached for guidance on

- personal/psychological issues (31.8 percent of the time)
- marriage/family/relationship issues (40 percent of the time)
- work and employment issues (37.7 percent of the time)
- senior-related issues (53.8 percent of the time)[18]

They also found "a high degree of mistrust and cynicism about the official church structures and officers, which usually were not perceived as being useful sources for one's own spiritual growth."[19] The clergy talked openly of their "loneliness, frustration with the ambiguities and stresses of the ministerial role, and a sense of never having enough time to attend to themselves, their families, and their own spiritual lives."[20] The researchers identified five principal needs in the testimony from these clergy:

1. greater clarity and integration of professional roles;
2. recognition and affirmation;
3. a place to be dependent and/or a person to depend upon;
4. a community marked by learning, trust, and affirmation; and
5. knowledge of and experience with spiritual disciplines.[21]

Just as in the study of Methodist clergywomen that will be noted in the next section, here the theme of a need for a safe place emerged. Like the Methodist women, these respondents expressed a strong desire for a place outside the normal denominational system. The respondents were looking for "a longer term, structured, high quality program which involves a continuing community of learners working together."[22]

Indicator 3: Retention of Women in Ministry

A further clue to the state of leadership in congregations is to be found in the presence and place of ordained women in congregations and systems that claim to welcome them. Margaret S. Wiborg and Elizabeth

J. Collier prepared their study on the retention of clergywomen in the United Methodist Church for the Anna Howard Shaw Center of Boston University School of Theology and, like the Klaas study, did so with financial support from the parent denomination. Beginning with a couple of troubling denominational statistics ("nearly one-third of United Methodist clergywomen in full connection were not serving local churches five years ago" and "women are leaving local church ministry at a ten percent higher rate than male clergy"[23]) the researchers set out to discover why their colleagues were exiting parish ministry.

Like most mainline Protestant denominations, the Methodists did not begin ordaining women until mid-century (1956 in the case of the Methodist Church, the major predecessor denomination that merged to form the United Methodist Church in 1968). This mid-century entry of women into ordained ministry was a major challenge to the Methodist denominational system, as it was to all others. Stories of glass ceilings, inequity in pay, and various kinds of harassment are a part of this dramatic challenge to the leadership ecology of American religion.

The study concluded with this single sentence: "They leave the local church primarily due to lack of support from the hierarchical system, a difficulty to maintain their integrity in the current system, family responsibilities, and rejection from their congregations."[24] Through this project the 1,388 women who completed the survey (out of a population of about 4,000), and the 123 who agreed to be interviewed, sent a strong message about a system that they did not trust and that caused them pain. Most painful in the report are the firsthand accounts of mistreatment—by congregations that cut salaries, clergy colleagues who called the clergywomen "little helpers," bishops who misrepresented congregations to the women clergy and the clergy to the congregations they were called to serve.

The report focused particular attention on the appointment system (which received a 74 percent negative response), on compensation inequities, and on bishops who functioned more like CEOs than like pastors. It also pointed out dysfunctional patterns among Annual Conference leaders and clergy colleagues. In particular, the researchers zeroed in on systemic flaws in the pattern of superintendency. On the one hand, the report argues, the *Book of Discipline* states that the superintendency "is supposed to be the space where clergy can go to receive guidance and counsel when needed." Yet, many of the women felt that this space was not safe for them because "the district superintendent also is responsible for the evaluation and appointment of the clergy in their district."[25] Congregational expectations were also a great problem these women encountered, receiving an 86 percent negative response. The report carries painful accounts of women who were told by parishioners that going on the youth ski trip counted as personal vacation time or whose personal lives were mercilessly scrutinized by church members. Many felt that their seminary education did not prepare them at all for the realities they encountered in local church ministry.

As we have seen in the Klaas study—which focused on poor clergy morale, modest levels of despair, and advanced stages of burnout— those surveyed referred to a "sick denominational system" as a contributing factor. Similarly, in the United Methodist Clergywomen Retention Study there was reference to dysfunctional patterns among Annual Conference leaders, to the flaws in the superintendency system, and to unsafe denominational space. Even the hopeful Episcopal Zacchaeus Project report (which will be cited in the section on ferment below), carried with it concerns about widespread confusion over the roles and functions of bishops and ineffectual and weak denominational structures.[26] It is clear from this evidence, that while clergy supply is a very pressing reality, we must also attend to the systems to which we are trying to recruit clergy.

Part 2: A Horizon of Ferment

While the dominant reading of the current situation casts a perception of crisis, there is in the current moment a sense of ferment that suggests transitions leading to hope, renewed energies, and a yet-to-be fully understood birthing. In 1978, historian William G. McLoughlin speculated that the period from 1960 to 1990 might one day be called "The Fourth Great Awakening."[27] He placed the ferment of the '60s and '70s into the longer story of "revitalization movements" in America. According to anthropologists who study cultural transformations, these movements simultaneously carry within them a crisis of legitimacy for the old order and an effervescence of new alternative spiritual expressions. Looking at his own time, McLoughlin wondered if within the stirrings of black power, Eastern religions, the counterculture, and neo-Evangelicalism were early signs of an awakening as important as the First Great Awakening (1730–1760) in reshaping our country's soul. It remains to be seen just how important this time of ferment will turn out to be—or if America will in fact be "revitalized" by the series of crises and the waves of ferment that continue to unsettle us. McLoughlin did not predict that this time of spiritual ferment would last as long it has. He did not anticipate all the new forms of religious community—including many within the Christian and Jewish worlds—that became more visible in the waning years of the twentieth century. But he did see, earlier than most, that America was entering a time of crisis and ferment that would fundamentally change it.

If anything, the changes that have occurred in the years between McLoughlin's writing and our own time have only intensified the effects of the transformations he identified. Mainline Protestantism recognized its "dis-establishment." New immigration laws set in motion changes that will result in the reversal of majority and minority statuses by the end of the twenty-first century as Hispanic and Asian peoples fundamentally alter the political and cultural realities of our land.[28] The computer and the Internet have radically democratized access to knowledge and have set the new electronic information-based economy into aggressive competition with the "old" manufacturing and service economies. America is in the midst of a leadership sea change in which old established leadership patterns are experiencing a crisis of legitimacy and new spiritual effervescence abounds.

The congregations of America—and the people who lead them—are simultaneously encountering great new spiritual vitality and a crisis of legitimacy of their established leadership patterns and practices. It is important to note signals of this strong and surprising vitality. For example, in 1999 the Episcopal Church Foundation published its Zacchaeus Project report. The report was unique for denominational research projects in that its primary data came from grassroots focus groups of lay members, rather than clergy. The Foundation found some good news for a mainline denomination accustomed to hearing a litany of woes about membership decline (from 3.5 million in the mid-1960s to 2.3 million in 1997), scandal (financial and sexual misconduct), and great institutional conflict. Here the news was "Episcopalians celebrate a powerful feeling of 'pulling together' with a sense of common purpose and mutual support." They found that "creative ferment and vitality characterize Episcopal life in local congregations" and that "a clear sense of shared ministry of both clergy and lay leadership in local churches has been an important fruit of the Episcopal Church's shift in emphasis over the past fifty years." Thus at the local congregational level these researchers found a surprising ferment.[29]

There are also sightings of vitality beyond the mainline, but each carries with it troubling leadership implications. In *Reinventing American Protestantism*, for example, sociologist Donald E. Miller looks at what he calls New Paradigm churches, in particular the new quasi-denominations or movements known as Calvary Chapel, Vineyard Christian Fellowship, and Hope Chapel. These new religious groups, along with better known megachurches like Willow Creek, are part of what Miller believes to be "a revolution" that is transforming American Protestantism. He asserts that, "While many of the mainline churches are losing membership, overall church attendance is not declining. Instead, a new style of Christianity is being born in the United States, one that responds to fundamental cultural changes that began in the mid-1960s."[30]

Ferment, for Miller, is abundant, but it is taking new institutional forms. When he looks back at the mainline Protestantism that nurtured him, the implications are ominous: "I see most liberal churches missing the mark: their message is ambiguous, lacking authority, and their worship is anemic. Furthermore, they are mired in organizational structures that deaden vision as people gather endlessly in committee meetings. . . . Given the level of creativity and innovative leadership among new paradigm Christians, I do not see how mainline churches can compete with new paradigm churches unless they radically reinvent themselves."[31]

Sometimes the ferment expresses itself outside of normal denominational and congregational structures. In another research project, Miller and several colleagues found a different kind of ferment, this time in terms of institutional creativity and civic leadership. In a study of the activities of congregations in South Central Los Angeles after the 1992 riots, they found evidence of stunning coalition building, spiritual entrepreneurialism, and civic leadership coming from local congregations. New not-for-profit organizations were coming to life in order to meet the deep social, economic, and health-care needs of a troubled and explosive community. As Korean, Anglo, Hispanic, and African American congregations worked together, a new "politics of the spirit" was creating a new "civic infrastructure" where none had existed.[32] Again, at the grassroots there is clear evidence of vitality, although this time of a different quality. But with these new institutions and the new entrepreneurs who create them come a new set of leadership challenges: How to sustain and support such efforts for the long haul? As our nation responds to the challenges of welfare reform and the new set of expectations placed upon congregations and other faith-based organizations by the U.S. government's Charitable Choice legislation, the new set of leadership challenges foreshadowed in Los Angeles multiply exponentially. These challenges will indeed deepen as congregations consider the new opportunities and responsibilities of ministry that now face them in President Bush's Faith-Based and Community Initiatives program, which invites faith communities to step up to new roles and relationships in their communities.

Much of this ferment flies below the radar screen of religious experts and leaders. It occurs at the edges, or outside of, or below the established structures that we have used to organize religious life in America. For example, another sign of ferment to note here is the emergence of "lay pastors" in a variety of American denominations. At present we do not know how many people are playing such roles in America. Although they may be called by different names in different traditions, essentially these new leaders are laypeople who are trained to exercise some or all pastoral duties in one local setting, often a small congregation unable to support a full-time, seminary-trained minister. A recent study discovered more than 158 judicatory-based study programs that have been developed to support these new leaders.[33] The emergence of this new leadership strategy—and of a large number of new programs to train them—is, on the one hand, a sign of ferment and institutional creativity. On the other hand, as the report makes clear, this new leadership role and the new educational process pose serious challenges to existing models of theological education and longstanding patterns of preparing people for ministry and credentialing them.

If we return again to an examination of ordained clergy as a bell-wether of the state of our congregational and denominational systems, there is also evidence of some ferment. Granted that the research base is spotty and that some of the studies may be disputed for methodological or political reasons, it nonetheless seems clear from the reading of crisis in the preceding section that the American clergy system is in pain. People do not feel safe in their clergy systems and they often feel alone and cynical about the systems that are supposed to support them. Nonetheless, one can easily find clergy who are thriving; these studies clearly point to them. For many, including those who are flourishing, these systems are problematic, as noted. Further, these beleaguered clergy systems are facing new stresses of under-supply and the many other challenges of postmodern (and, perhaps, post-denominational) religion. But religious sociologist Nancy Ammerman, for example, has concluded from her recent studies of American denominations that some clergy and congregational leaders are finding new and meaningful connections to their denominations. Those who do must confront the erosion of denominational culture and must be intentional about constructing new denominational identities—a skill frequently untaught in the seminary.[34] What she observes is part of a larger historic development that historian E. Brooks Holifield has described as a movement from the minister as colonial officer in the seventeenth and eighteenth centuries, to the minister as either professional or populist leader in the nineteenth century, to the minister as generalist or specialist in the twentieth century, to the minister in a time of transition and confusion about role at the start of the twenty-first century.[35]

Finally, consideration of the leadership situation facing congregations must include attention to the leadership role of lay members of our congregations in the worlds in which they live, work, and play. This great throng of people, the largest group of members of any type of voluntary organizations in this country, has become accustomed to a wide range of new leadership models and roles. They are better educated than any previous generation. Many of them recognize that the time has long passed since clergy were the only learned ones in the community and laypeople were dependent upon them. Helping these people identify their leadership roles as members of congregations and then helping them carry their religious beliefs and values out into the

world as resources for leadership is a challenge of huge proportions—
especially when the leadership infrastructure of their congregations is
under such stress.

Part 3: The Alban Institute's Position

At the grassroots level, where much of the Alban Institute's
work is done, we find many signs of ferment in our own connection
with congregations and their leaders. Congregations are growing, and
in very new ways. New generations are coming into many established
congregations, often making their presence felt with new preferences
and practices. It is not uncommon—in fact, it is more typical—for us
to work with congregations where the group of members and participants who have been in that congregation for less than 10 years rivals
or exceeds the size of the group of members who have been in that
congregation for more than 20 years. We see this as evidence of healthy
and vital congregations that are reestablishing themselves in their communities with a new "generation" of participants.

While certainly not reversing the well-known trends of declining
denominational memberships, such grassroots evidence of ferment is
making a difference as some denominations are at least noting an increase of attendance at worship, if not membership. For example, the
Episcopal Church noted that despite their decline in membership, average attendance increased by 31 percent between 1974 and 1997, measured by averaging the attendance at the "Four Key Sundays" during
the year.[36] This increase was in contrast to the 25 percent increase in the
general population during the same period. Similarly, the United Methodist Church reported six consecutive years of U.S. attendance increases
and noted that in 1998 the average Sunday attendance increased by
13,000 persons.[37]

We have watched congregations jump in worship attendance as
much as 40 percent within months by adding worship services sensitive to their surroundings. We have worked with congregations to learn
new ways of making decisions and dealing with differences because of
their success at welcoming diversity and becoming truly inclusive. We
have worked with skilled clergy and lay leaders in congregations that
often do right and healthy things intuitively as leaders in complex set-

tings. And we have consulted with, trained, and learned from committed and creative judicatory and denominational leaders who often find themselves in the very systems accurately described as dysfunctional in the earlier part of this report but who are aware of the problems and committed to making a difference.

These are days when many in our society are looking for new leadership from members of our religious communities. Our government is asking faith-based organizations and local congregations to step forward and lead in an era of devolved governmental welfare. Social commentators like David Brooks are challenging the most affluent and best-educated generation in human history, the boomers, to do one thing that they have not yet tried—take a leadership role in the refurbishing of our public life. The affluent people he calls the Bobos (shorthand for Bourgeois Bohemians), who reconciled one of the deepest divides in modern life by bringing together the cultures of the Bohemians and the Bourgeoisie, have ended up with small moralities and spiritualities of complacency.[38] As Brooks seems to recognize and as others plainly see, it is this vast group of privileged Americans, many of whom have found their way back to church, that also needs new kinds of resources to lead a culture in search of its soul. What Alban does in helping to create these resources must unite practical solutions to practical problems with an understanding of the deep, sustaining sources of imagination and wisdom.

Standing on the Side of Ferment

In this report we are recognizing the necessity of risking a seemingly paradoxical perspective on the current state of the leadership situation facing American congregations. That paradoxical perspective must include an awareness of *both* turmoil *and* ferment held in responsible tension. In our exploration it has become clear to us, as it must be to the reader, that the tension is clearly tipped toward turmoil for many, if not most, of the people and the sources that we consulted. It would not be responsible to ignore this sense of crisis that has been at least partially documented as a description of our current predicament. But it would be equally irresponsible to be insensitive to the ferment that is already at hand and to fail to look for creative ways to respond to this changing landscape of American religion and congregational life. We do not deny there is a crisis; however, we do assert that in the attention given to the crisis are signs of ferment that indicate that the crisis will be addressed in new and creative ways.

It is the conviction of the Alban Institute that leaders must learn to hold the paradox of turmoil and ferment in hand, but to stand on the side of ferment. The vision for leadership of both laity and clergy in our congregations and congregational systems must be more than problem solving. The leaders who are needed to respond to the ferment that is building must have a passion for the values and truth that they find in their faith and a conviction that leaders have a voice of spiritual imagination that needs to be heard in the larger community as well as in the congregation. We are past the place of understanding spiritual leadership as a distinct role to be played within the structures and programs of an institution. Our congregations are beginning to seek people of substance and preparation that will allow them to speak the imaginative word of leadership within the broader public of which the congregation and its members are a part and in which the congregation can be seen as the platform from which the voice of faith-based leadership of clergy and laity alike can be heard.

In our historic commitment to resourcing and preparing leaders of congregations, the *Alban Institute clearly takes its stand on the side of ferment.* For us this means being even clearer about not committing our resources simply to fixing old problems and discomforts that will only return our systems to levels of false satisfaction that mirror a time prior to our current moment of paradoxical tension. It also means following the current evidence and emerging hints of the new ferment that calls for new leadership and the preparation of those leaders. We stand looking for partners in that emerging work.

Making New Leaders: Identifying and Working the Challenges

In light of the seemingly paradoxical realities of sea change and crisis, of ferment and turmoil, those who lead congregations—as well as those who support congregations in judicatory, denominational, seminary, and independent roles—face an important set of challenges. The recruiting, training, and support of new leaders require major changes in our assumptions, behaviors, and the systems in which we live. Among the most important challenges are the following:

1. We need to develop new, healthy, and safe environments for clergy to learn and connect. There is abundant evidence that the old denominational systems are, for many, not providing the support, the safety, and the resources that leaders need. New spaces, both within and beyond denominational and seminary systems, need to be invented. Denominations, seminaries, and other leadership institutions in American religious life must create environments and structures that encourage leaders to take risks and that are capable of sustaining leaders when they experience failure. A key part of this challenge is amassing venture capital to support new experiments and new learning environments.

2. New pathways and processes of learning need to be created for all congregational leaders. Clergy and lay leaders need supportive peer learning environments, educational programs, and resources that are richly interdisciplinary in settings that enable them to negotiate the many boundary crossings that are required in contemporary culture and in most local congregations.

3. All of these leaders need to see leadership in new ways. Their vision and imagination about their callings and roles need to be opened. They must be equipped to read the culture critically, to read their congregations carefully, and to read their theological sources creatively and faithfully. They must learn a new set of adaptive skills that allow them to shape new patterns of congregational life and new leadership roles. And they must be helped to integrate the various kinds of knowledge and experience that flow through their lives and the lives of the people they serve.

4. There are many leaders who feel dispirited or ill-equipped for their current roles. A variety of resources—remedial, organizational, ethical, and theological—need to be available

to help people learn in ways appropriate to their actual
settings. And, where people no longer have the capacity to
serve as leaders, we need to provide clear exit routes.

5. Major attention must be given to recruiting the next
   generation of leaders. Special efforts must be made to reach
   young people with compelling images of the leadership
   challenges and opportunities awaiting them in congregational
   life. Great attention must be paid to removing the major
   systemic barriers that discourage their consideration of such
   roles.

Conclusion

The Alban Institute feels called to make these realities and
concerns, in all their paradoxical richness, its central work in the coming years. We know that this set of challenges is much too large for us—
or for any congregation, judicatory, seminary, or denomination—to
attempt to resolve single-handedly. Rather, we hope to identify others
who wish to grapple with these issues and to find new and creative
ways to work together to address them.

The challenge before us in a time of sea change is to shift from preoc-
cupation with institutional problem solving to a new commitment to
capturing people's imagination and providing wellsprings of hope. To
make this shift requires a new calling of leaders, a new training of leaders, and a new supporting of leaders, both clergy and lay, who can stand
with poise and fidelity in both the crisis and ferment of this great sea
change.

Bibliography

"Academic Preparation of Master of Divinity Candidates," *Ministry Research Notes* (Fall 1990).

Ammerman, Nancy T. "New Life for Denominationalism," *The Christian Century* (March 15, 2000), pp. 302–307. Available online at hirr.hartsem.edu/bookshelf/ammerman_article3.html.

Appleby, R. Scott. "Surviving the Shaking of the Foundations: United States Catholicism in the Twenty-First Century," in Katarina Schuth, ed., *Seminaries, Theologates, and the Future of Church Ministry: An Analysis of Trends and Transitions* (Collegeville, Minn: The Liturgical Press, 1999).

Barker, Lance R., and B. Edmon Martin, *Alternatives in Theological Education: An Examination of the Characteristics and Outcomes of Denominational Judicatory Study Programs which Prepare Persons for Commissioned, Licensed, Ordained or Otherwise Authorized Ministries* (New Brighton, Minn.: United Theological Seminary, 2000).

Brooks, David. *Bobos in Paradise: The New Upper Class and How They Got There* (New York: Simon and Schuster, 2000).

Castelli, Jim, and Eugene Hemrick, *National Catholic Parish Survey: The New Church Emerges* (Fairfax Station, Va.: Castelli Enterprises, Inc., 2000).

Chaves, Mark. *How Do We Worship?* (Bethesda: The Alban Institute, 1999).

"A Crisis in Leadership: A Letter to the Middle Governing Bodies, General Assembly Entities and Theological Institutions of the PC (USA)," *The Presbyterian Outlook* (September 25, 2000).

Eck, Diana L., *A New Religious America: How a "Christian Country" Has Become the World's Most Religiously Diverse Nation* (San Francisco: HarperSanFrancisco, 2001).

Evangelical Lutheran Church in America, *Ministry Needs and Resources in the 21ˢᵗ Century* (Chicago: Evangelical Lutheran Church in America, 2000). Available online at www.elca.org/research/reports/dm/minstudy.pdf.

Hess, Kurtis C. "Trends & Transitions Facing the Church" (Unpublished report, 2000).

Holifield, E. Brooks. "The Clergy," in *Encyclopedia of American Social History* (New York: Scribner, 1993), pp. 2465–2472.

Holland, Thomas P., and William L. Sachs, *The Zacchaeus Project: Discerning Episcopal Identity at the Dawn of the New Millennium* (New York: The Episcopal Church Foundation, 1999). Available online at www.episcopalfoundation.org/leadership/Zacchaeus.

Klaas, Alan C., and Cheryl D. Klaas, "Clergy Shortage Study," (Smithville, Mo: Mission Growth Ministries, 1999).

Lord, William, and John C. Bryan, "Project on the Spiritual Development Needs of Mid-Career Clergy: Report of Findings" (Toronto: Toronto School of Theology, 1999).

McLoughlin, William G. *Revivals, Awakenings, and Reform: An Essay on Social Change in America, 1607–1977* (Chicago: The University of Chicago Press, 1978).

Memming, Rolf. "United Methodist Ordained Ministry in Transition (Trends in Ordination and Careers)," in William B. Lawrence, Dennis Campbell, and Russell Richey, eds., *The People(s) Called Methodist: Forms and Reforms of Their Life*, United Methodism and American Culture, vol. 2 (Nashville: Abingdon Press, 1998), pp. 129–130.

Miller, Donald E. *Reinventing American Protestantism: Christianity in the New Millennium* (Berkeley: University of California Press, 1997).

Orr, John B., Donald E. Miller, Wade Clark Roof, and J. Gordon Melton, *Politics of the Spirit: Religion and Multiethnicity in Los Angeles* (Los Angeles: University of Southern California, 1994).

The Reconstructionist Commission on the Role of the Rabbi, *The Rabbi-Congregation Relationship: A Vision for the 21st Century* (Wyncote, Penn: The Reconstructionist Commission on the Role of the Rabbi, 2001).

Wheeler, Barbara, "Is There a Problem: Theological Students and Religious Leadership for the Future" (New York: Auburn Center for the Study of Theological Education, 2001). Available online at www.auburnsem.org/images/publications/pdf_8.pdf.

Wiborg, Margaret S., and Elizabeth J. Collier, "United Methodist Clergywomen Retention Study" (Boston: Boston University School of Theology, 1997). Available online at www.bu.edu/sth/shaw/retention/.

Wicai, Hillary. "Clergy by the Numbers." *Congregations*, vol. 27, no. 2 (March/April 2001).

Notes

1. A sample of those initially interviewed include: Daniel O. Aleshire, executive director, Association of Theological Schools; Jackson Carroll, professor, Duke Divinity School; Craig Dykstra, vice president for religion, Lilly Endowment Inc.; Walter Fluker, director,

Leadership Institute at Morehouse College; Terry Foland, senior consultant, Alban Institute; Michael Gilligan, program officer for theology, Luce Foundation; Kirk Hadaway, director of research, UCC Board of Homeland Ministries; Chris Hobgood, regional executive, Christian Church (Disciples of Christ); David Hubner, ministerial development director, Unitarian Universalist Association; Jack Johnson, United Methodist district superintendent; Glenn Matis, Episcopal priest; Paul Menitoff, executive vice president, Central Conference of American Rabbis; Steve Ott, director, Center for Career Development and Ministry; Janet Peterman, ELCA pastor; Leonard Thal, vice president, Union of American Hebrew Congregations; David Wolfman, regional director, Union of American Hebrew Congregations; and Mary Wood, Episcopal priest. Each of these individuals spoke freely and frankly with us. We assured them that, while we would make use of the substance of their responses, we would not attribute any quotations to them without their permission.

2.   R. Scott Appleby, "Surviving the Shaking of the Foundations: United States Catholicism in the Twenty-First Century," in Katarina Schuth, ed., *Seminaries, Theologates, and the Future of Church Ministry: An Analysis of Trends and Transitions* (Collegeville, Minn.: The Liturgical Press, 1999), p. 2, n. 1.

3.   Jim Castelli and Eugene Hemrick, *National Catholic Parish Survey: The New Church Emerges* (Fairfax Station, Va.: Castelli Enterprises, Inc., April 2000), pp. 1–2.

4.   Rolf Memming, "United Methodist Ordained Ministry in Transition (Trends in Ordination and Careers)" in William B. Lawrence, Dennis Campbell, and Russell Richey, eds., *The People(s) Called Methodist: Forms and Reforms of Their Life*, United Methodism and American Culture, volume 2 (Nashville: Abingdon Press, 1998), pp. 129–130.

5.   Evangelical Lutheran Church in America, *Ministry Needs and Resources in the 21st Century* (Chicago: Evangelical Lutheran Church in America, 2000), pp. 3, 8. Available online at www.elca.org/research/reports/dm/minstudy.pdf.

6.   Mark Chaves, *How Do We Worship?* (Bethesda: The Alban Institute, 1999), p. 8.

7. Kurtis C. Hess, "Trends & Transitions Facing the Church," (Unpublished report, January 2000), pp. 1–3.

8. Hillary Wicai, "Clergy by the Numbers." *Congregations*, vol. 27, no. 2 (March/April 2001), p. 9.

9. "A Crisis in Leadership: A Letter to the Middle Governing Bodies, General Assembly Entities and Theological Institutions of the PC (USA)," *The Presbyterian Outlook* (September 25, 2000), pp. 10–11.

10. The Reconstructionist Commission on the Role of the Rabbi, *The Rabbi-Congregation Relationship: A Vision for the 21st Century* (Wyncote, Penn: Reconstructionist Commission on the Role of the Rabbi, 2001), p. vi.

11. With the exception of the GRE scores, these statistics come from the ATS 1999 Graduating Student Survey, which Daniel Aleshire graciously made available to us. The GRE statistics come from "Academic Preparation of Master of Divinity Candidates," *Ministry Research Notes* (Fall 1990).

12. "A Crisis in Leadership."

13. Memming, "United Methodist Ordained Ministry in Transition (Trends in Ordination and Career)," pp. 130, 144.

14. Barbara Wheeler, "Is There a Problem: Theological Students and Religious Leadership for the Future" (New York: Auburn Center for the Study of Theological Education, 2001), p. 3. Available online at www.auburnsem.org/images/publications/pdf_8.pdf.

15. Alan C. Klaas and Cheryl D. Klaas, "Clergy Shortage Study," (Smithville, Mo: Mission Growth Ministries, 1999), pp. 47–48.

16. Ibid., pp. 56–65.

17. PastorCare mailing.

18. William Lord and John C. Bryan, "Project on the Spiritual Development Needs of Mid-Career Clergy: Report of Findings" (Toronto: Toronto School of Theology, 1999), pp. 1–2.

19. Ibid.

20. Ibid.

21. Ibid., p. 27.

22. Ibid., p. 36.

23. Margaret S. Wiborg and Elizabeth J. Collier, "United Methodist Clergywomen Retention Study" (Boston: Boston University School of Theology, 1997), p. l. Available online at www.bu.edu/sth/shaw/retention/.

24. Ibid., p. 57.

25. Ibid., p. 43.

26. Thomas P. Holland and William L. Sachs, *The Zacchaeus Project: Discerning Episcopal Identity at the Dawn of the New Millennium* (New York: The Episcopal Church Foundation, 1999), pp. 10, 15. Available online at www.episcopalfoundation.org/leadership/ Zacchaeus.

27. William G. McLoughlin, *Revivals, Awakenings, and Reform: An Essay on Religion and Social Change in America, 1607–1977* (Chicago: The University of Chicago Press, 1978), pp.179–216.

28. See Diana L. Eck, *A New Religious America: How a "Christian Country" Has Become the World's Most Religiously Diverse Nation* (San Francisco: HarperSanFrancisco, 2001).

29. Holland and Sachs, *The Zacchaeus Project*.

30. Donald E. Miller, *Reinventing American Protestantism: Christianity in the New Millennium* (Berkeley: University of California Press, 1997), p. 1.

31. Ibid., p. 187.

32. John B. Orr, Donald E. Miller, Wade Clark Roof, and J. Gordon Melton, *Politics of the Spirit: Religion and Multiethnicity in Los Angeles* (Los Angeles: University of Southern California, 1994).

33. Lance R. Barker and B. Edmon Martin, *Alternatives in Theological Education: An Examination of the Characteristics and Outcomes of Denominational Judicatory Study Programs which Prepare Persons for Commissioned, Licensed, Ordained or Otherwise Authorized Ministries* (New Brighton, Minn: United Theological Seminary, 2000), p. 11.

34. Nancy T. Ammerman, "New Life for Denominationalism," *The Christian Century* (March 15, 2000), pp. 302–307. Available online at hirr.hartsem.edu/bookshelf/ammerman_article3.html.

35. E. Brooks Holifield, "The Clergy," in *Encyclopedia of American Social History* (New York: Scribner, 1993), pp. 2465–2472.

36. Holland and Sachs, *The Zacchaeus Project*, p. 57.

37. *The United Methodist Newscope,* vol. 27, no. 48 (November 26, 1999).

38. David Brooks, *Bobos in Paradise: The New Upper Class and How They Got There* (New York: Simon and Schuster, 2000).

The Leadership We Need: Negotiating Up, Not Down

GIL RENDLE

Perhaps, when Abraham sought to save Sodom by interceding on behalf of the city, his attempt was rooted in the Hebrew tradition of trusting in the presence of 50 righteous men to provide salvation. But he was not assured that the full count of righteous ones could be found, so he negotiated down: "Suppose 5 of the 50 righteous are lacking? Will you destroy the whole city for lack of 5?" And he (the Lord) said, "I will not destroy it if I find 45 there." Pressing his advantage, Abraham negotiated further, asking for reprieve if only 40 were found, then 30, then 20, and then finally 10 until the Lord answered "For the sake of 10 I will not destroy it" (Gen, 18:22-33).

Minimizing Expectations

A number of voices in the American religious landscape would suggest that Abraham might be the model for what has happened in congregational leadership over the past years as we have negotiated our expectations down to minimal levels. Indeed, have we negotiated our expectations of congregational leadership down to such a minimal, or at times and in places, less than functional level that the leadership no longer serves our congregations well?

In recent months, the Alban Institute has surveyed the landscape and uncovered a good deal of episodic research that suggests that the

Originally published in *Congregations,* vol. 27, no. 5 (September/October 2001): pp. 4–7.

news is not good. In many quarters major clergy shortages are being reported, and the stream of seminary graduates who actually intend to serve as parish leaders will be insufficient to replace those planning to retire.

Questions are also being raised about the quality and competence of those, both clergy and lay, who are serving as leaders in our congregations. When compared with applicants to other graduate professional academic programs, seminary applicants register some of the lowest test scores. Even our healthiest leaders do not feel equipped to address the spiritual questions and concerns of their people; a large percentage of professional clergy evidence symptoms of burnout or depression. Our most gifted lay leaders often feel a stronger call to serving on community boards and participating in non-faith-based programs where they feel a clearer sense of purpose and accomplishment.

More complete reports on the state of congregational leadership and our processes for preparing people for leadership are offered elsewhere, including the Alban Institute Special Report on Leadership. I propose simply that we consider our own loss of the meaning of spiritual leadership as a contributing factor to the current situation. I would argue that we, like Abraham, have negotiated our hopes and expectations down because we have not been assured of the high calling of leadership in a faith community

Diminished Leadership Roles

The feared and frustrating description that I learned early in my own parish leadership was the trap of being "overworked but underemployed." Do we have people who do not rise to the challenge of congregational leadership because they understand that "busyness" is not an indicator of importance? More troubling, do we have people who do respond to this call because they understand that nothing of measurable importance will be asked of them, and the congregation therefore feels like a safe place to step forward in the leader's role?

I would suggest that the role of leader in the faith community has been diminished in several ways, of which I would point quickly to three. First, spiritual leadership has been trivialized into institutional

management, a role beleaguered by the multiple preferences and factions that exist in congregations unable to find satisfaction. Second, we
have placed our spiritual leaders in a false intermediary position between our own needs as we have defined them and a God whom we
assume to be available but increasingly insignificant in a world dominated by the promises of technology And third, we have limited our
spiritual leaders by expecting them to be the models and personifica-
tion of civil behavior and cultural moderation that others feel free to
choose or reject in their daily lives.

Our expectations about spiritual leadership have become unclear;
we project onto them, as we do onto the therapist's professional neu-
trality, all our individual wants, needs, preferences, and complaints. This
lack of clarity regarding our expectations of leaders becomes mirrored
in the confusion of those who feel called to that role. Reflecting the
experience of other faith traditions, the recent report of the
Reconstructionist Commission on the Role of the Rabbi notes,

> A decreasing number of rabbis and rabbinical students, in all streams
> of North American Judaism, intend to seek positions in congrega-
> tions. They cite concerns about schedule, boundaries in personal and
> professional life, employment security, compensation, the complex
> nature of the diverse responsibilities that comprise congregational
> work, and the consequences for physical and emotional health of be-
> ing on-call at all times....The work of the congregational rabbi has
> evolved in ways that make the job simply overwhelming and unwork-
> able for many rabbis.[1]

Unclear roles and expectations make our leaders subject to everything
without significant responsibility for anything.

Valuing Spiritual Leadership

Have we negotiated our expectations down because we have
not known what to ask of importance from our spiritual leaders? We
have asked for trivial, unrealistic things. We have not valued spiritual
leadership and therefore have rewarded our leaders poorly. We have

ended with calls for leadership in which the workload is great but the challenge is small.

Perhaps the adventuresome, worthwhile response would be to negotiate our expectations of leadership up, not down. What if we risked an assumption that spiritual leadership is important? What if we believed that faith centered on a relationship with God has something significant to say to us in our work lives, families, marriages, friendships, and communities? Such a belief would certainly be countercultural—it would mean standing independent from many current cultural assumptions and adopting a perspective different from the prevailing scientific worldview.

Truth with Meaning

"There is arguably no more important and pressing topic than the relation of science and religion in the modern world," says philosopher Ken Wilber in the opening lines of *The Marriage of Sense and Soul.* Science is clearly one of the most profound methods that humans have yet devised for discovering truth, while religion remains the single greatest force for generating meaning."[1] Yet ours is a moment when we seek ways of holding both truth and meaning. This then is a time to assert clear expectations that leaders who can frame meaning have a word of importance to say

In order for meaning to stand equal to truth we need to call, prepare, support, and reward leaders who can speak the word of meaning in the midst of multiple, and often competing, truths. This is, in fact, the role of prophetic leadership in the Old Testament sense of seeing what everyone else sees but identifying and pronouncing the hand of God where others seek simpler explanations.

Using Wilber's culturally forced dichotomy of science and religion— of truth and meaning—we can see also the related but distinct leadership roles of specialist (science) and generalist (religion). If we are to negotiate up our expectations of our spiritual leaders we will need to call and respond to people who are "deep generalists." Corporate consultants Jagdish Sheth and Andrew Sobel define a deep generalist as someone who has a core expertise onto which he or she layers knowledge of related and sometimes unrelated fields.[3] While that may sound a bit dry and detached, it speaks of having a very deep knowledge of one's own truth but also having sufficient insight, maturity, experience, and wisdom to be able to maintain an informal, generalized approach to complex situations. For a spiritual leader it means being able to stand deeply in one's faith while functioning broadly across multiple areas and experiences of life to bring new understanding, direction, and hope to those who are led.

Seeing New Realities

I consider Harrell Beck, who taught Old Testament wisdom literature at Boston University School of Theology, to be such a deep generalist spiritual leader. A friend and mentor to me in my early years of ministry, Harrell taught classes for which one needed to be a middler or senior at the seminary in order to gain a prized place on the roster. But despite the limit to the number of class participants (usually around 20), the room was routinely filled with an additional 25 to 40 students who would come simply to hear Harrell's opening prayer before the teaching began. The prayer would focus on the life of the seminary but reach out to include issues of the city and events of the nation and world. At the conclusion of prayer a few moments would be given to allow non-class members to file out, and then the teaching would begin.

Always amazed at his prayers and the response that he evoked in so many of us, I remember asking Harrell how he understood so many things so clearly that he could address not only our own community but also issues and events that it took whole newspapers to chronicle. His response was the simple but disciplined truth of the deep generalist spiritual leader. Harrell quickly admitted that he did not understand all that I ascribed to him. "But I do understand wisdom literature," he said. "And I can talk about what the world looks like when you look through the lens that God has given us in the Old Testament." He stood deeply within the discipline of his faith, but he was able to move broadly across life experience. I wonder what our congregations would be if we had more such leaders who stood deeply in their understanding of the faith and had the ability to help us see new realities in our own experience of life.

Valuing New Gifts

What if we negotiated our expectations up and called deep generalists of faith as our leaders in congregations? Costs and challenges would be involved. We would need to move outside of cultural norms to value the strange gifts our new leaders would bring. Those leaders would need to be exceptionally mature and able to stand out-side of cultural norms, knowing that their gifts are valuable.

For example, our culture gives time, place, and speech to the specialist who holds some word of truth. Consider how one must go to the office of a physician even for visits requiring none of the equipment at that office, and how waiting rooms are often filled with people whose time is assumed to be less important than the physician's. In a recent visit to a medical specialist I was interrupted whenever my answers did not go where the physician felt necessary and the physician only gave clear information when challenged. Clearly speech was assumed to belong to him.

To the contrary, deep generalist leaders must be mature and centered people who understand that they are to listen as the more important part of conversation and that speech belongs to the one who has the need. Deep generalist leaders understand that they must go to the place where the person is faced with need—to the hospital bed, the home, the lunch meeting, the committee meeting, the unexpected confrontation in the community. Deep generalist leaders understand that timing belongs to the other and that the word of meaning cannot be spoken until the time is ripe for listening.

There is a personal and relational cost to be paid by deep generalists of meaning who can stand maturely and securely in a culture that more naturally rewards specialists of truth. There is also the cost of preparation that must be paid by those called to this most unique of leadership roles.

Seminary training for clergy and adult Bible and faith study for laity are only the entry points for these leaders. They learn the faith deeply not just to teach others but, more importantly, to be able to stand deeply within a perspective that allows them to see and announce the world from the very different perspective of faith.

But the learning must continue. Leaders must learn the culture in order to speak to it, a task with purpose much deeper than market research and sensitivity They must learn the particular congregation in order to vision with the people. They must learn the lives, the professions, the events of their people in order to bring faith meaning to their experiences. Perhaps most difficult, they must learn themselves in order to stand in relationship with, but free of limiting dependence on, others. To call, prepare, and support such spiritual leaders bears the heavy cost of rethinking and redesigning the ways in which we will train and evaluate them.

Abraham negotiated his expectations down in the hope of saving Sodom. We too have tried this with our expectations of congregational leadership, only to discover that we have lost what we hoped to save. Hope comes not in negotiating down to meet minimal requirements. Hope comes in raising our expectations of spiritual leadership. Hope lies in challenging gifted and risk-taking people to a place of leadership of meaning based on faith. Hope lies in our own willingness to receive and reward leadership that may in fact, change us.

Notes

1. *The Rabbi-Congregation Relationship: A Vision for the 21st Century* (Philadelphia Reconstructionist Commission on the Role of the Rabbi. 2001). pp. 1–2.
2. New York: Random House. 1998, p.3.
3. Jagdish Sheth and Andrew Sobel, *Clients for Life: How Great Professionals Develop Breakthrough Relationships* (New York Simon & Schuster, 2000), p 87.

Leading from the Bottom Up: Bureaucracy and Adhocracy

HOWARD FRIEND

I have worked with a number of churches who have revitalized themselves through a steady and consistent focus on lay vocation.
However, these promising episodes of energy and new life could remain just that—an ebb and flow of episodes. To maintain their vitality,
these churches must become institutionalized in the best sense of that
word. They must explore new forms of governance. Yet everywhere evident are the sad and discouraging stories of decline in a vast majority
of mainline denominational churches, clinging to traditional modes of
governance. Despite their familiarity, these old forms of governance
simply don't work as they once did. Heartening, however, are emerging
new forms that, though less easily understood and still a-birthing, are
potentially far more powerful in their ability to transform a congregation into what it discerns it is called to become.

An ocean voyage demands the courage to lose sight of the land of
departure long before catching a first glimpse of one's destination. Centuries ago, such exploration could feel like "sailing off the map." Today,
our churches face a journey of similar uncertainty. Trustworthy maps
of the new governance forms that will better support congregational
life are yet to be fully and accurately drawn. But, carrying the old maps
of traditional governance under one arm and the still sketchy and uncertain maps of the new under the other, we must journey forth into
uncharted waters if our churches are to have any hope of discovering
the new life they seek.

Originally published in *Congregations*, vol. 31, no. 2 (Spring 2005), pp. 6–11.

What we are facing is not the *developmental* type of change we see in a tadpole's gradual, orderly, incremental, and fully visible transformation into a full-grown frog, but the much more mysterious *transformational* change we see in the transition from caterpillar to butterfly. Few people realize that inside the chrysalis the caterpillar has wound around itself is a bundle of formless cells, a puddle of protoplasm, neither a caterpillar sprouting wings nor a husk soon to drop away revealing a butterfly. All that the caterpillar was and all that the butterfly will be are contained in the chrysalis, but one form must relinquish itself that another might emerge. This kind of change is mysterious, hidden, and full of surprise—and a far less comfortable process of change than that exemplified by the tadpole. This kind of change is revolutionary. It is seemingly chaotic, disruptive, disorganized, and out of control—not likely our choice for how we'd like to experience change.[1] But it may well be that we need to affirm and even welcome this kind of change if we are to see life return to congregations in decline.

The Bible is crammed with verses and narratives that echo this theme. Indeed, the foundational event, the defining metaphor of our faith, is not resuscitation but *resurrection*, the ultimate transformation.

Building on Rock

Nevertheless, the old ways can provide support for such a resurrection, as the following story illustrates: A creative young pastor was called to a traditional but faltering small town church. He combined a passion for the creative and innovative with keen sensitivity and a pastor's heart. The church had a sturdy and devoted core of longtime members. Many of them were descendents of a few families who had loved and served the church for decades, and they were vigilant guardians of the traditions. But the engaging style and contagious energy of the new pastor soon attracted a growing number of newcomers. He began to make changes—gently, he hoped. Young adult programs sprang up. Different types of music were added to the worship service. A youth program grew, swelled by previously unchurched community teens. The lights were on in the church almost every night of the week! But from one longtime member came a candid and revealing complaint: "It feels like us old-timers are being pushed off the table." The young pastor's response was inspired: "Well, I guess we need to build a bigger table!"

That creative, bridging response became public. "Both/and" thinking dispelled the fears generated by "either/or" assumptions. The "new table" strategy was able to maintain and celebrate the old while still openly embracing the new. Too many first-call pastors roar into the church armed with exciting but untried templates of congregational renewal, leaving members feeling under siege. Likewise, experienced pastors often return from a workshop on revitalization, their enthusiasm for sweeping changes overwhelming the congregation's startled leaders. Many of these ministers then react with surprise and resentment to the understandable and predictable resistance to their proposed changes. Recalling that Jesus came not to abolish but fulfill, and that he advocated the building of houses on rock can help strengthen our faith that the new can rise on the solid foundation of the old. This wisdom can be seen in the following, similar stories of three different churches.

A Streamlined Infrastructure

A Methodist church, among the larger of six congregations in a mid-sized east coast city, after two decades of steady decline, experienced a sudden season of renewal under a new, energetic pastor with solid preaching credentials, a contagious enthusiasm, and an engaging vision. An ambitious building program was initiated, membership increased by a third in less than five years, and the church's newsletter constantly featured new opportunities to learn and serve. The organizational infrastructure, with its proliferation of new committees and endless additional meetings, was not only cumbersome and unwieldy but also out of alignment with both the content and spirit of all that was happening. More than just alteration and adjustment were needed; a complete overhaul seemed in order. Six months later, participation and ministry were still burgeoning and new programs were multiplying, but the total number of standing committees had been reduced from 29 to 8!

From a Pyramid to a Circle

A United Church of Christ church decided to stay at its center-city location in a deteriorating New England city even after the last of the
other congregations in town had relocated to the suburbs. Their building a burden, their membership in decline, and once thriving programs
dwindling, crisp vision and pesky determination persisted. A strategy
of encouraging new groups and ministries to "bubble up" naturally
proved immediately promising, but those tasked with maintaining an
administrative structure inherited from the congregation's glory years
grew restless. Ultimately, they dared to jettison the whole bulky affair.
They combined three boards into one, replaced the typical organizational pyramid with a circle, and reduced the number of committees
and meetings by two-thirds—all as new programs, small groups, educational opportunities, and mission efforts flourished.

A Focus on Empowerment

In a stable, established suburban community, a small, liberal congregation in the shadow of several thriving tall-steeple churches wondered
about its future. Facing discouraging demographics and unable to compete with the vast program offerings and large staffs of the big churches,
it decided to re-invent itself, becoming, by intention, a niche-market
congregation. Consciously shifting paradigms proved helpful. If the large
churches were like supermarkets, with a product to meet every need,
they'd become a farmer's market, providing space where programs and
ministries emerging from member initiative could be offered. If the
large churches were like catered banquets with endless buffets, they'd
be like a covered dish supper. Leaders and standing committees began
to encourage rather than sponsor new programs, and to empower rather
than provide new ministries. In the process, they reinvented governance.

The organizational map of each of these churches emerged and
evolved individually, but came to look something like the diagram on
the next page. Each wanted to be intentionally and decisively Christ-
centered and biblically-grounded (thus the cross at the center of the
diagram). Each had a circle of mission-focused and goal-oriented
boards and standing ministry teams (the *bureaucracy*). And the vital-

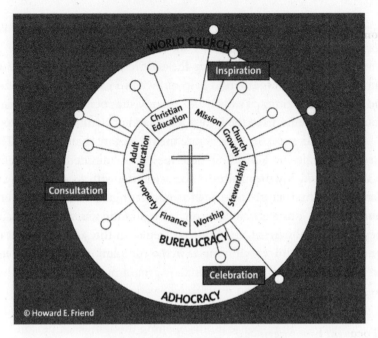

A New Map of Church Goverance

ity of the church—the ever-broadening number of groups, programs, and ministries—occurred in the outer circle of activity, the *adhocracy*.

Three Levels of Renewal

If we take a closer look at each congregation's journey, we will find common threads. Three levels of renewal serve as a foundation on which to build.

Renewing the Meaning of Membership

If you join a Rotary Club, a friend recently told me, you attend 80 percent of the weekly meetings and choose the project to which you will commit time, energy, and money. "No exceptions?" I asked. "No exceptions." I've been a volunteer fireman in two communities. You attend meetings, go to fire school, show up at drills, and fight fires. That's that. But ask an average member of a congregation what membership in the church means and it's a different story: "I guess I oughta go to church,"

they mumble, with "oughta" being the defining word—heavy with ob-
ligation, thin on joy. "I suppose I should send a check from time to
time" likely follows, barely lifting the needle on the Richter scale of
commitment. "I guess I should help out when I can" limps in third—
and when a call comes, it's likely not perceived as being the right time.
Churches, it seems, have the lowest membership standards in town!

But churches seeking to revitalize themselves are changing that. The
self-styled niche-market church described above decided to replace its
legacy of casual, low-bar attitudes about joining with a six-month new
member orientation process. Each participant, accompanied and encouraged by a "spiritual companion," now attends courses and classes,
keeps a personal journal, and is introduced to the life and ministries of
the church. This process culminates in the completion of the following
three-part New Member Covenant:

- *Because I want to deepen my faith and my relationship to God, I
  will* . . . . In response to this opening thought, each person
  crafts a "spiritual growth discipline," typically including
  commitment to regular worship, a daily devotional practice,
  joining a small group, and attending programs or workshops
  (or helping to initiate a new spiritual support group or
  program).
- *Discerning my calling and gifts, and knowing myself to be a part
  of the Body of Christ, I will serve this church by* . . . . Guided in
  this discernment and introduced to the array of opportunities
  to serve, each new member finds his or her place or, as often
  as not, links with others in the class to create new
  opportunities for service.
- *Believing that a Christian is called to make love and a
  commitment to peace and justice visible and concrete in the
  world, I will* . . . . By completing this thought, each person
  commits to a clear and specific plan for sharing his or her
  faith, living a vigorous personal and relational ethic, and
  advocating for peace, justice, and the poor. Almost every class
  has developed at least one new mission outreach effort.

While there was resistance to this bold change at first, the fruits of the
new approach included increased numbers of people desiring to join,

appreciation for the process, and an infusion of hearty and sustained participation and serving by new members—and, it turned out, a renewal of commitment by longstanding members. Membership covenant writing became an annual ritual at the turn of the year. This church would likely affirm that its most important job description is its *member* job description.

Creating an Intentional Nominations Process

All too aware of the frustrations of board member recruitment, a nominating committee member may quietly muse, "How small do I have to make this job to get a yes?" Persuasion yields to pleading, the operative criteria being to *get this job done quickly*. But when discernment of calling and giftedness is the foundation for member responsibility-taking and serving, it is logical to approach nominations similarly. Imagine that same recruiter with a new script: "I am calling for the nominating committee. We have been pondering and praying, assessing our vision and goals for the year ahead, and sharing the names of those we sense are called, gifted, and ready to serve in leadership. I am calling to invite you to serve on our official board and to chair the Mission Committee. We have noticed your passion for outreach and your faithfulness in serving on several committees. I know, as an officer myself, that this task will demand significant time and energy. You may need to consider pruning your commitments in other areas to give this work full attention. It is a high calling. I do not ask you to give me an answer now. May I call back in about a week? In the meantime, feel free to call me with any questions. And please know, though we offer this invitation with full confidence and hope you will accept, that we want you to discern what feels truly good and right for you. Feel free to accept or decline, as you feel led." Callers who take this approach find, to their surprise and delight, that they get heartier and more durable commitment and, yes, more yeses.

Developing an Effective and Efficient Bureaucracy

Each of the churches described earlier tightened, sharpened, and streamlined its *bureaucracy* in the positive and creative spirit of that word. Organizational units were typically eliminated or combined. Board,

committee, and leader job descriptions were crafted to artfully combine autonomy and accountability. The congregational vision statement
was regularly revisited and renewed; each ministry team created a mission statement to guide its work, projected goals for the year, and for-
mulated an action plan to carry them out; and leaders were trained in
the skills necessary for effective leadership—all in a spirit of sharing
and celebration. Bureaucracy is not a bad word.

Welcoming the Brand New—Adhocracy

In the process of streamlining their bureaucracies, these
churches found themselves reinventing governance. They shed the all
too prevalent and pervasive view of leaders as people "elected to do the
work," adopting instead a partnership vision of a leader: "a *person* who
works with *people* to accomplish a *purpose*," redefining leaders as people
who work *with* rather than *for* the membership. They moved away from
the typical "producer-consumer relationship" between leadership and
membership, where leaders offer "products" (programs, groups, events,
etc.) and hope members will "buy." Rather than polling members about
their needs so they could offer appropriate programs and opportunities to serve, leaders encouraged and equipped groups of members large
and small to create their own opportunities for service. The familiar
operational mantra, "*You come on in,*" where leaders beckon the membership to "come join our committee or ministry team, come out to
support our programs, come and help us with our work," becomes
"*We'll go out* into the membership, helping folks with creative ideas
for programs and ministries mold and shape them, helping people
with similar callings to link up, form a circle, and put wheels under
those ideas." This approach involves "self-directed people on self-
managed teams," as Stephen R. Covey, author of *Principle-Centered
Leadership*, puts it. Top-down governance is replaced by bottom-up
governance.

Notice that the largest space on the graphic shown on page 45 is
beyond the bureaucracy—in the adhocracy. That's where the action is.
Even the church walls cannot contain it! As the *bureaucracy* shrinks, all
the while becoming more effective, the *adhocracy* blossoms. Ultimately,
in the three churches described above, three-quarters of the programs,

events, and opportunities appearing on the churches' monthly calendars and in their newsletters were member-initiated, autonomously structured grassroots programs and ministries. It's important to note that this approach was not, for these churches, merely a strategy—an innovative and outside-the-box tactic—or some new governance technology carefully applied. It was, first and foremost, an expression of faith, a product of foundational convictions such as the following:

- Human beings naturally long for the divine.
- There's a deep, inborn desire to deepen and grow in relationship to God.
- The church as the Body of Christ, a priesthood of all believers, compels everyone to find their place.
- The church belongs to the people.
- People are to be encouraged to discern their calling and giftedness for serving and then manifest these calls and gifts.
- Naming the vision, mission, and goals of the church is the work of corporate discernment.

New governance this may be—with all the prayerfulness, creativity, and courage it demands—but it is firmly rooted in faithful conviction.

The Two Hats of Leadership

Let's return for a moment to the aforementioned Methodist church in the mid-sized city. A longtime, beloved but rather autocratic pastor had departed and the congregation found itself in a season of transition—perhaps toward the more partnership-based model of governance the new minister advocated. A new identity, a fresh vision, and a revitalized sense of mission seemed poised to emerge. The staff and key leaders went on a retreat. The exchanges were vigorous, but at times the differing visions for the church seemed competing, even colliding. "Who are we? What do we want to be?" the youth minister asked. "Are we a supermarket or a mega department store? Or a giant home center?" a lay leader added. "What if we are to become a *mall*?" the Christian educator mused. Something clicked! "A mall has two or three anchor stores, like worship and Christian education and pastoral care, then a whole lot of smaller stores," the lay leader added, building the momentum.

The mall metaphor offered coherence and cohesiveness while affirming variety and multiplicity. The congregation's basic approach to church growth and its organizational map came to look like our graphic. The *bureaucracy* developed and managed the "anchor stores": property, worship, finance, Christian education, and so on. The lay leaders donned "manager hats." But that's only half of the job! A second hat is called for!

Developing and nurturing *adhocracy* demands an additional, different kind of leadership, which may be a truer form of leadership than what we typically see in churches. It's important to keep in mind that the *adhocracy* is an *approach* to expanding program and ministry; it does not directly create them. This is dramatic, sweeping, transformational, caterpillars-to-butterfly leadership. More than new thoughts or new ideas, this kind of leadership demands *a new way of thinking*.

Three Leadership Functions

So how can one best introduce this new approach? How can a congregation shift its initiative for programs and ministries to the membership? How can this energy and responsiveness be motivated from the bottom up? It may involve three basic roles and functions for leaders: inspiration, consultation, and celebration.[2]

Inspiration

How can congregational leaders create and nurture an environment of initiative and responsibility-taking by laity, an environment of inventiveness and creativity, of motivation and responsiveness among the membership? How can leaders "get the word out" that all can be co-creators of the ministry of the church? These questions begin to turn the soil in this region we are calling *adhocracy*. Inspired and inspiring leaders create and nurture a climate of expectancy, of responsibility-taking, of eager lay initiative. If you could read the congregational journal of that niche-market church, you'd see it unfold—slowly at first, haltingly, tentatively, almost imperceptibly. Indeed, let's use them as a model. Here are some illustrations of how the adhocracy of that church developed—with inspiring results:

- Sara met an Episcopal priest from Haiti, and wept as he spoke of the children in the most depressed part of Cite Solei (City of the Sun). She heard how little money it took to sponsor a child's primary education, and compassion was transformed into action. *Scholarship Solei* began when three families each pledged the $200 yearly tuition and uniform costs for a student, another committed the $950 salary for a teacher, and yet another wrote a check for $1,500, which built a simple cinder block school.
- Jeff, the part-time youth and outreach minister, practiced his Spanish as he talked with the Galo family from Nicaragua during their residency for a week at the church. He learned that owning a bicycle could be the key for high school graduates to begin their university education, and coaxed the congregation's teens into rounding up old bikes and coming to youth group an hour early to repair them. This, in turn, infected the congregation with the dream. The church sent its thousandth bike to Nicaragua not long ago!
- Bill didn't find any of the church's existing adult education options appealing. Challenged to start his own, he invited others to join him in "praying over the news" as he spread out the Sunday paper in the church's kitchen after worship each week. His circle became a steady, dedicated half dozen.
- Jay didn't want to join the property committee but said he'd plant and tend the gardens by the entrance. The idea caught hold and soon every garden on the church's property had a sponsoring family.

Three years later, the number of the church's programs, groups, and ministries had tripled in number and participation. Three-quarters of them had been initiated in the *adhocracy*. Other churches have adopted a similar approach with similar exciting results!

Consultation

People with fresh ideas and a readiness to carry them forward need assistance: guidance, encouragement, coaching, and access to resources, including budget. People leading a hands-on mission might seek out the Outreach Committee chair. Someone with an adult education idea might connect with the Christian Education Committee. These leaders know how to "get beside" the people who can best assist them *while keeping the ball in their own hands*. In the transformation of the New England congregation described earlier, the annual budget included "undesignated funds" for both education and mission outreach, so programs could birth anytime during the church year. Mini-courses or one-on-one consultations were available to teach the skills needed to birth a new ministry: convening and empowering a group, setting an agenda and leading a meeting, focusing vision and setting goals, and making appropriate contacts outside the church. Sometimes it was as simple as "Here are keys to the church. This is how you turn on the lights and adjust the heat" and "There are the folding chairs and coffee supplies." Paul would call it "equipping the saints."

Celebration

Leaders of empowered congregations are "liturgists of celebration." People need, want, and have a right to recognition, affirmation, and celebration, so write newsletter articles, feature a ministry or program each Sunday, use them as sermon illustrations, or put a photo collage on the bulletin board. Create a climate of appreciation not just for the "successes" but also for devotion, commitment, and hard work, even for initiatives that didn't work so well. Celebrate faithfulness; it is a way to remember that it is God who "works it all together for good."

Making the Crossing

New governance is a work in progress. It's emerging and evolving. Moses and Isaiah remind us "to watch for the new thing God is doing among you." Martin Luther invites us to love God and fail boldly. A two-week walk from the Red Sea crossing to the Jordan crossing took 40 years! But in that Jordan crossing is an inspirational metaphor for new governance. In that story, Moses had made his last speech and climbed Mount Nebo to die. Less formidable than the Red Sea, the Jordan was still a body of water to be crossed. Joshua called the people to the bank of the river, asking that the leaders stand in the front. "Just begin walking into the water," he instructed. The narrative suggests that the waters toward the future parted "as they walked." No dramatic parting after a single step, yet slowly, steadily parting with each step that was taken.

Those who would be church leaders, dare to stand in front . . . and start walking!

Notes

1. This metaphor builds on the work of Harrison Owen, *Spirit: Transformation and Development in Organizations*, (Potomac, MD: Abbott Publishing, 1987), 7–9.
2. See Howard E. Friend, *Recovering the Sacred Center* (Valley Forge, PA: Judson Press, 1998), 143–149.

What Does It Take to Lead a Congregation Today?

HOLLIS R. WILLIAMS, JR.

How has ministry changed over the past twenty-five years?
In a changing church how is the pastor's role evolving?

Two years ago I celebrated the twenty-fifth anniversary of my ordination to the priesthood. It caused me to reflect on the manner in which things had shifted over the past 25 years. The church has certainly changed and there is an evolving new role for the ordained minister. Authors I read in the areas of environment, new biology, and business talked of a shift of consciousness in the world. What they wrote described the way I was experiencing the culture around me and my perception that being in the church seemed different now and brought new challenge. The model of church and priesthood for which I had been trained did not exist anymore. It was as if the job description had been rewritten or I had been transferred to a new department one Monday morning!

Recently I have spent some time reflecting on what it takes to be a pastor today, to preside over and give leadership to a congregation in the 1990s. A group of friends continue to ruminate with me around this question, and I offer these thoughts for your reflection and response. I happen to be an Episcopalian, but the same dynamic seems to be going on in other denominations. I hope you will respond with experience and insight from your own ministry.

Originally published in *Congregations,* vol. 21, no. 2 (March/April 1995): pp. 17–19.

For me the local congregation continues to be the locus of church life and mission. It remains the basic unit for communicating the Gospel in the community, whether rural, urban, or suburban. Basic to pastoring today is an ongoing affirmation to serve the local congregation and to see its promise, its importance, and its strategic opportunity for penetrating the surrounding world with the love of Christ. There are other ministries and opportunities in which one's vocation as an ordained person can be exercised, but the local congregation is a primary focus for mission and ministry today. To be pastor of a congregation today requires personal clarity, ability to listen, some new skills, and openness to fresh resources to enrich and stretch gifts for leadership. Here are some things I think help make for a satisfying pastoral experience in a congregation.

Know Your "Gifts" or Strengths

What do you do best? Most of us are generalists, sometimes with a focus in a particular area, but more often not highly specialized. However, within your general ministry you may be sharper in biblical studies, pastoral care, crisis ministry, liturgy, or education. What areas of education and experience are the strongest in your skill bank? What is your editorial slant, bias, passion about the tradition? Define yourself around these interests in the context of a congregation. Do ministry out of these gifts with clarity, energy, and intention. That is where you have competence and strength. There may be areas important to the congregation that are not your strongest skills. It is important to be open and honest about this with laity. Work together to discover a way to meet those needs. (Otherwise the expectation will remain for you to meet them.) Mutual clarity and mutual problem solving can go a long way in preventing the deficiencies from falling entirely on your shoulders and enable shared ministry which will strengthen the entire body.

Make a Good Match:
You and Your Congregation

Each congregation is unique. That is one of the important insights to come out of the studies of congregational systems and dynamics. Each congregation has its own history and personality. The interview process is the time to sharpen your focus on the picture of the congregation. Read between the lines when studying profiles. Take note of impressions of what the building and grounds communicate when you drive up, enter, walk through them. What can you find out about the place? What is it like to live there? Trust the visceral messages. What are the needs for leadership at this time in the life of the congregation? Are your gifts and interests congruent with those opportunities? I feel that the call happens best when the needs of the congregation and skills of the clergyperson intersect like a dovetail or finger joint in a fine piece of furniture. In the dialogue that develops there may be energy, confidence, and sharing. If it is confirmed by the Spirit, a good match emerges that has vocational potential. Being pastor is more than a job. It takes more to thrive, even survive, as pastor of a congregation today.

As one settles in as pastor, ongoing contact with the remembered history is important for incarnational leadership. Storytelling about the high and low moments in the life of the congregation is often incredibly revelatory. Listen to the stories of the past. Once is never enough, for often important new information is revealed when the story is told again or told by another elder. These stories can give important clues to historic and ongoing issues, ways of dealing with life, attitudes about change, the nature of authority, and faith perspectives in the congregation.

Relationship Is Primary for Effective Pastoring

The central message is that God cares. The congregation is a community of care. Caregiving is a part of pastoral ministry. People expect the minister to be interested in others and care about them. It is even more important today than in the past that the congregation knows that the minister cares about them and their lives. Shepherd, not hireling, is the image in John's Gospel. Today so many clergy feel that they are treated as hirelings, especially as the business model of clergy placement is acted out in so many of our church calling processes. If people know the pastor is interested in them, cares about them and their lives, and loves them, then the pastoral bond is established. That bond can

diminish the hireling dynamic and all the undertow that goes with it.
After all, clergy still have access to people in the peak experiences of life.
To be there, to stand with them, and to follow through with attention
not only from the pastor but from members of the congregation is the
essence of pastoral ministry. This bond is central to the covenant "I will
be your God and you will be my people."

Stay Healthy

Choose a lifestyle that keeps you well. There is a growing
collection of literature that affirms important habits for the ordained
person. To be a healthy person one needs balance between work,
leisure/play, family and nourishing relationships, and worship. That
balance is a priority in order to stay fresh for thoughtful program and
pastoral leadership. It doesn't take much overwork to become physi-
cally and spiritually thin and consequently ineffective. Regular exercise, physical activity, and games are important to personal well-being.
The biblical perspective on the integration of mind and body is on
target. A healthy body improves the mind; a good mental attitude fuels
the body. Time for family and primary relationships nourishes the spirit.
It is often most valuable to have some primary friends outside the
church, people you enjoy and in whose presence you can be natural
and authentic without the overtones of role evaluation. Care of the
soul through personal worship and spiritual refreshment undergirds
all of life. A group of spiritual friends, a spiritual director, or personal
retreat deepens the relationship with the Holy One—a necessity for
those who lead others in worship. A regular time for prayer and meditation connects us to the Holy One who is making all things new all
around us. Maintaining the relationship with the Holy One and staying in communion with spiritual friends is a rhythm that enhances
staying power.

Other areas of self-care that promote health are worth mentioning
in the environment in which vocation is lived these days. Rapid and
continuous change impacts us. Both the church I signed on with and
the role of ordained person continue to evolve. With change comes loss
and with any loss the dynamics of death and grief must be faced and

lived through. Only then can we emerge in a different space and live comfortably and hopefully. The feelings that can surface in the midst of change are naturally a part of us. They must be honored and processed to allow time for internal healing and thereby prevent the anger and burnout that can surface in relationship with others. It is important to be in touch with the impact of change going on within ourselves and be open to God working within that to lead us through it to a new perspective. A spiritual friend always reminds me and others to "do your own work." For him that means processing one's personal and vocational "stuff" with a support group, spiritual director, or therapist. Self-knowledge and personal and spiritual growth enable us to be sharper about personal relationships and our boundaries as pastoral resource. It can help avoid the relationships that are potentially unhealthy for our ministry.

Be a Bearer of the Vision of the Kingdom

Jesus came preaching that the kingdom of heaven is at hand. We have come to know and catch a glimpse of that in the transforming love of the risen Christ. Leadership in the context of today's congregation requires vision. The pastor is one who stimulates and drives the people of God in a particular place toward a vision of the kingdom. It is developed out of the partnership in the Gospel between pastor and people. The process involves laity and clergy praying, studying, and working together in community to discover what God is calling them to be and do.

The vision process has some important pieces. It begins with dialogue and careful listening. The immediate goal is to establish trust and create a comfortable environment where the faith and perspective of each person can be shared. That process builds a reasonable and accurate picture of the values, hopes, natural gifts, and energy of the congregation. Then leadership is involved in refining and shaping that information together with the congregation into a sharper focus for mission and ministry. It is built on the strengths, opportunity, and energy of the saints in that place. This process enables lay leadership to claim ownership for the excellence of the church and the future

ministry of the congregation. The pastor gives permission for this process, encourages it to happen, contributes as an active and equal part-
ner with the congregation and its leadership. The pastor also serves as
the living reminder of this vision and the implications of it for the
mission and ministry of the congregation in all facets of its life. It is an
ongoing process of listening, reflection, dialogue, and action for the
whole congregation, pastor and people, to be accountable for the Gospel in that place.

Authoritarian leadership, the old top down kind of management,
doesn't wear well in these times. People want to be involved, to be in-
vested. Authoritative leadership, a style that engages others in moving
forward with an opportunity, is needed in church and culture. No one
organization can be dependent on one person to bring all that is needed.
People seek to be included in shaping the institutions and organisms of
which they are a part. They have good ideas. The church is entrusted to
them by God and guided temporarily by their pastor. Leadership is
more important than ever, but a different style of leadership is what is
needed in the church. For a congregation to grow spiritually there needs
to be a partnership between pastor and people. Each respects the other
and brings gifts, vision, and effort to develop and carry forward the
mission of the church in that place. Strength builds on strength. Our
congregations today need leadership that is visionary, collaborative, and
authoritative.

Teach, Explain, and Interpret

Many people who are coming to churches today have little
or no background in the faith. They don't know the story. They might
hear or use phrases and references to biblical concepts, but have no
knowledge of what they mean or where they came from. Even the regu-
lars could benefit from being refreshed on the basic details of the story.
It is a time to reach back to the roots, to the essence of the Gospel, to
the basic building blocks of faith and tradition. The task of recovering
the basics of faith and biblical themes for daily living in our churches
cannot be dismissed as a "conservative agenda." There just can't be too
much ongoing teaching and interpretation. Dick, Jane, and Spot for
Christians may be the rule in parish education for the next few years.

Some Closing Thoughts

You need to keep on growing in knowledge of yourself and knowledge of your parish in order to share your gifts, your vision, and your passion effectively. With the increasing diversity of people in church and society today, a lively sense of humor helps you savor the variety of emotions and expectations in church life, promoting sanity and enhancing your capacity to enjoy relationships with the congregation.

There continues to be a hunger for the spirit in our society. Meet that hunger by giving people what they expect—good worship, lively music, meaningful liturgy, interesting preaching, and inclusive prayer. The quality of what happens on Sunday morning has never been more important. Improve your skills, build upon your resources, and strive for balance. These are challenging and difficult times. As you face the storms without, keep inner peace by strengthening your relationship with Christ and with a small group of associates. Do not be surprised when the dark side of human nature surfaces. You will encounter both authentic kindness and deviousness in parish life; expect both. Do not be overwhelmed when pettiness sparks clashes. The Bible and church history are filled with vivid illustrations of the glory and misery of human nature.

Take responsibility for your ministry. Attitude is almost everything. There is too much complaining and blaming in institutions, especially in the church. Wake up every morning with this perspective: God is good, the church is good, people are good, the bishop or judicatory head is good. Massaging the flaws distorts us from the primary task of being faithful in the present moment and pointing to the kingdom that is always coming. We are in a significant shift in the church. The task ahead is to discern what is essential, define what is not essential (though important to others), and put aside that which is truly trivial.

Action and Reflection:
A Rhythm of Ministry

ART GAFKE AND BRUCE McSPADDEN

Week after week, the story was the same: a man on a white horse rode into town just in the nick of time and saved the day. As the crowd gathered, the noble hero dug his heels into his trusty steed's side, the horse reared up to full height, and the man directed "Hi ho, Silver, away!" and disappeared into the sunset. The episode ended as a whisper rose up from the admiring crowd. "Who was that masked man?"

What pastor hasn't wished to be like the Lone Ranger, that fond hero from childhood who knew exactly how to rescue every troubled situation? Everyone would like to act nobly, yet ministry is no place for lone rangers who act heroically but then disappear until the next crisis. And yes, people in the church sometimes seem to want a superhero for a pastor; however, simply going from one crisis to the next doesn't work for true-to-life leaders. Another ministry rhythm that allows for purposeful action, meaningful reflection, and personal renewal is needed.

The Gospel accounts reveal that Jesus was a dedicated healer and teacher who regularly pulled away from the crowds, despite their constant crisis demands, to be with the few he trusted most and also to be completely alone to pray and reflect in order to be renewed. His life rhythm of action followed by reflection is one that is essential for the long-term health and success of anyone involved in ministry.

Many pastors prefer to act. You know the type; she's the one whose church started the community food program and organized the peace

---

Originally published in *Congregations,* vol. 19, no. 1 (January/February 1993), pp. 3–6.

rally during recent military action. She's the one the media calls upon for sound bites in times of community upheaval because everyone in town has heard of her. Her actions are admirable and good, but after attending her parish for a while, congregants begin to wonder what the underlying mission is that ties all of these actions together.

Other pastors love personal reflection. He's the kind of pastor who can be found daily, hour after hour, in his study intently preparing next Sunday's sermon. But when soldiers were sent oversees and readying for action, the pastor's sermon said nothing about it. When a terrible flood devastated many houses in a nearby county, there was nary a prayer or act of practical assistance offered. All too often his sermons seem to emanate out of the wise pages of good books, but rarely do they touch the people where they hurt.

Both of these pastors could benefit from adopting a rhythm of action and reflection. In order to do so each one must embrace five assumptions about ministry.

We are in covenant with each other. A pastor who acts justly is no more grounded than the one who reflects deeply if neither of them is closely and regularly in dialogue with his or her congregation. The Christian faith is both a personal and communal faith—our personal actions and beliefs are influenced and guided by our participation in the body of faith.

Three foci help pastors integrate ministry and guide reflection. The reflective pastor considers: in what ways do I empower people, extend covenantal relationships, and build the church? These three questions are invaluable in structuring a pastor's reflective process in the midst of the disparate tugs and demands of ministry.

Reflection fuels right action. Do we believe that the events in our life and world are random happenings or part of the ongoing revelations of God? Too often we fail to think about the events in our personal lives and local communities. Too often services or special programs are offered by a church, but no one stops to evaluate if or how well they served the long-term mission of the church. Understanding that events, conditions, and interests in people's lives fuel their actions allows the church to harness people's energies to better the whole community.

Power is found in building relationships of mutual trust. Two heads are truly better than one. Two hands at the plow can cover more ground than one working alone. A pastor who understands that his or her role is one of empowering the congregation through developing trustworthy relationships with a few leaders who then extend themselves to others who do likewise will build a powerful, growing church.

Accountability is a requirement of balanced ministry. Even the Lone Ranger had Tonto, the one who always appeared by his side as they rode off into the sunset. Everyone needs people in his or her life who will offer feedback, insight, and support throughout the ups and downs of life. Ministers must have an accountability system to thrive. And accountability measures are most supportive when they are personally sought out, self-initiated. Shaking hands at the back of the church on Sunday morning will not provide the kind of accountability that leads to honest reflection and right action. It is a ministerial right and privilege to find others who will regularly speak the truth in love.

Tools for Personal Reflection

Doubtlessly, most pastors will agree that we are bound in covenant to one another, that reflection fuels action, that empowering people builds the church, and that accountability is essential. Yet amidst the hectic pace of multiple services, innumerable committee meetings, weddings, and funerals, they may honestly ask, *How do I fit interpersonal reflection into my schedule and upon whom do I call?*

Here are a few suggestions.

Start with the people you see regularly. Perhaps you haven't thought to stop your church's lay leader after you've chaired another meeting to ask, "How did I do? Do you have any suggestions on how I can better facilitate this meeting next month?" If you ask with sincerity and an honest desire to learn, most people will gladly offer helpful feedback and move beyond simply stroking your ego. Ask, listen, then incorporate the helpful feedback into your next actions. People who invest time in the church care deeply about your success. When people see that you take their feedback seriously, they will freely offer more constructive input as time goes on.

Seek out and gather regularly with other pastors. No one can understand your difficulties and add perspective like another person in similar circumstances. Pastors can choose either to view each other as competitors or teammates. Weekly sessions for reflecting together on the problems and pains of ministry can provide strength when the inevitable times of being at odds with any congregation arise.

The value of this type of disciplined reflection cannot be overemphasized. In one western city a pastor was accused of moral misconduct. For months her congregation was split with some believing her and others holding fast to rumors. Her leadership was being undermined. Luckily this woman had joined a support team of pastors. During this horrible time, she was able to share her pain unedited. The group listened, supported, and helped her wade through the heavy emotional waters until she could refocus on what she wanted to accomplish in her church. By using her colleagues to gain perspective she was able to stay for two more years during which she cleared her reputation and completed the ministry goals she had come with to the church.

A neighboring pastor in the middle of a church conflict put together a slate of parishioners to replace a deadlocked church board and presented it to church members for a vote without consulting anyone in advance. His nominees were soundly rejected and the old board gained even more strength. Six months later this pastor called his bishop and without taking a breath outlined what he felt his options had been over the past months of difficulty. He was determined to resign. The bishop called some key parishioners and found out that the minister was not closely in relationship with anyone. The congregation didn't want their pastor to resign, they simply wanted to be included in the plans and dreams for their church.

Mentors or teachers can offer a broadened perspective of ministry. Some denominations pair new ministers with mentors and upon occasion these relationships work well. However, the responsibility of finding a mentor rests on the shoulders of each pastor. Mentors or teachers need not be people that one sees weekly. Meeting two to four times a year with a person who provides an in-depth evaluation of a pastor's actions and aids in developing a strategy for the future can make an enormous difference in keeping one's ministry focus clear.

The important aspect of this type of reflection is that it is focused on the pastor's needs. While the mentor implicitly receives benefit, the purpose of meeting is to prioritize the personal and professional concerns of the pastor.

Specialized counselors, spiritual directors, vocational counselors, or community organizers can be a source of counsel. These professionals can offer essential reflective help during particular passages in one's personal and professional life.

One pastor involved in an inner city ministry faced a difficult board meeting. He had decided forcefully to declare the injustices he saw being done by church policy. But before he acted, he phoned a community organizer with whom he worked. The organizer helped him to diffuse the emotional fog and identify what the pastor really wanted to accomplish at the meeting. Together they came up with a structure, direction, and agenda for the meeting that would accomplish the goal of unmasking the injustices without inflaming or alienating the board members. After the meeting a euphoric pastor called the organizer and recounted the commitment to change that was resolutely affirmed by the whole board.

Tools for Congregational Reflection

Adopting an action/reflection rhythm for ministry begins with the pastor but must not end there. The habits of reflection can be incorporated into the fabric of church life.

Here's how.

Recognize that nothing the church does is an end in itself. Every service, funeral, event, or meeting is an occasion for building community over time. The entire life of the church offers the opportunity for continuous leadership development.

For instance, church meetings require more than gathering a group of people. Effective meetings are enhanced if they begin and end with a time of reflection. At the onset an agenda for the meeting is discussed and adopted. A few minutes before the allotted time is spent, an opportunity for evaluating what the meeting has accomplished should be offered.

Additionally, the most effective meetings are preceded by a pre-meeting of the leadership to identify what needs to be accomplished and to support the leaders. Sound meeting strategy also includes post-meeting debriefing with participants. Taking the time to reflect regularly with people helps strengthen leadership, keeps vision clear, and opens creativity. Listening to the experience of those involved serves to validate people's involvement and keep the pastor and leadership closely tuned in to the congregation.

Make time to reflect with church leaders and encourage them to do likewise with those they serve. Many pastors report that the most involved lay leaders tell the pastor not to spend his or her time making pastoral visits on them. After all they see the pastor constantly in the midst of church activities. This advice, while meant to lessen the pastor's burdens and free the pastor for outreach, serves instead to short-circuit the process of community building. At least twice a year the pastor needs to sit down individually with major leaders for reflection about the person's life and leadership. This allows the pastor and church leaders to update each other on personal needs and prayer concerns. If a pastor or ministry leader is out of touch with the core leadership in the church, relationships will eventually disintegrate. Staying in touch demands less energy than having to restore communication.

Build in reflection times for volunteers. In most churches volunteers give unselfishly of their time and may or may not receive adequate thanks for their efforts. All too often people show up, work hard, and then go home without the opportunity to reflect on what happened.

Ministry leaders can effectively foster congregational reflection by linking together ministry partners. A church with ten children's church school teachers organized five ministry pairs for debriefing after each class. This simple pairing served to honor each teacher's experience and allowed two people effectively to pass on helpful feedback and suggestions to church leadership.

In one church the nominating committee took on the responsibility of contacting every person elected to church office to hear how their faith and lives were enhanced by giving leadership in the church. The committee also learned how the church could be helpful to its leaders. For a church to thrive, the self-interest of its leaders and members must be understood and addressed.

Find ways to bring outside perspective into the church. Churches can easily become insulated, closed systems because of the fear of risk and loss. Such fear is real but can be overcome. An objective, reflective eye can observe things that those involved are too close to see. Consultants hired to assist church leadership in program evaluation and strategic planning often challenge procedures or assumptions that have been long unexamined and accepted without question.

Outside perspective can also be achieved by encouraging church leaders to visit other churches occasionally with the intent of seeing how other groups achieve similar goals. One local church in the process of refurbishing an educational wing sent two trustees to visit a church in another town that had inexpensively transformed their old church basement into a brightly painted, inviting educational facility. The trustees came home with ideas that substantially decreased the amount of money they initially thought was needed to provide their church with updated classrooms.

The Long-term Benefits of the Action/Reflection Rhythm of Ministry

Times of pastoral change provide the prime examples of the benefits of an action/reflection rhythm of ministry. When a lone ranger pastor leaves a church it is not unusual for programs to decline. Parishioners wait for the new pastor to rescue and reassure them. In a church where action and reflection are practiced, active ministry continues even in times of pastoral vacancy and transition.

When listening and reflecting are built into the very fabric of church life, people know their efforts, opinions, and experiences matter. When people know they are valued, they stay involved, grow in leadership, and invite others to join their community of faith. The church, rather than being pastor dependent, becomes a dynamic place where people act together, listen to each other, and strengthen their gifts and talents to better further the mission of the church.

A church that acts and then reflects rarely needs a lone ranger. A hero from afar isn't the answer to the problems of the church. Collectively, acting and reflecting while encompassed by God's grace, we are the ones who embody Christ's presence now.

When Consensus Fails

DONNA SCHAPER

In seminary I learned always to work for consensus. Likewise, I learned never to take a vote. There is nothing wrong with voting when a discussion has brought differences to the surface. Still, consensus—the group "nod" that means we know that we agree and don't need to vote—can be a pleasant gift to community if and when it is possible.

Constitutionally, I tend to agree with people. I like harmony, dislike conflict, and have a personality that wants to smooth edges wherever I go. I feel that everyone has something to contribute, and thus I try to include every point of view in whatever statement I issue on any subject, even the matter of what is for dinner. My own children will confirm my tendency to say yes to whatever anyone wants to eat for dinner and then not to know what to do when they all want something different.

Three Churches in One

I have had to learn new behaviors. My very diverse Miami congregation refuses to agree on anything. Indeed, there are three congregations in one here, with different tastes, opinions, and cultures. One is the "little church across from the country club" where everyone knows everyone else. That church is friendly and not flashy; it does not need

Originally published in *Congregations,* vol. 29, no. 2 (Spring 2003), pp. 34–36.

hired soloists and has difficulty handling diversity. Another is the "choral cathedral" of the arts: anything less than a million-dollar pipe organ is not good enough for the musical tastes and desires of this parish. These parishioners resent the little church's thriftiness and lack of sophistication as much as the little church resents their luxurious tastes. The third church is the "outer galactic church of the edge" (we came up with these names ourselves), which cares more about outreach than either music or fellowship and thinks that arts programs should be shelved in favor of assistance to the poor.

No third of the church has enough respect for any of the others. Members often publicly insult each other. When we needed to carry out an accessibility project involving a wheelchair ramp, the "professional" types of the choral cathedral wanted to do it to ADA (Americans with Disabilities Act) code. They wanted to obtain city permits. The "populist" types of the little church were insulted: they thought that all the donated time they had given over the years was being disparaged. This anger managed to delay the project for seven months. Two men—one in a wheelchair, one not—remain angry at each other.

The Sound of a Church Splitting

One very sensitive financial issue was decided by a 16-15 vote after 31 meetings in which 35 people regularly participated. The issue concerned the church's endowment and whether it should be managed internally or externally. Internal management won the day, but this has allowed the people who preferred outside, professional management to pick away at those who chose the old-fashioned way of doing church business—without paying a fee. In this and many other matters, there is no right answer. Professional management of large sums of money that are to be given away in grants is a good thing. Likewise, congregational participation and hands-on volunteerism are good things. Competing goods demonstrate our diversity, over and over again.

I wasted a good bit of leadership energy on developing consensus. I sometimes let issues remain in discussion for five or six meetings, hoping that consensus might arrive. I also internalized a lot of anxiety about my consensus "tool" not working. It really did bother me when people insulted each other in meetings. It really did bother me that they thought it had to be "their way or the highway." I could hear the church splitting in my heart. And I was just as willing to make macaroni and cheese, red spaghetti, and chicken all for one meal as I had been at home with my now-grown kids. I was convinced we could do something for everyone. But the diverse factions chose against such compromise and abundance; none wanted the other to be pleased.

Learning to Love the Vote

When it became clear to me that consensus had failed—that we could not keep people happy even with three different dishes on the table—I realized that I had to change my behavior and leadership style. I wish I had changed sooner; it took me almost two years to let go of my hope for consensus and the underlying hope for diversity.

You can teach an old dog new tricks. Thus, while I grieved for harmony in diversity, I changed my behavior. First of all, I learned to love votes and to take them with a smile on my face. Then I discovered that the majority of the people were not on the edge of these separate congregations so much as in the middle of them. Only a few in any of the three identifiable circles were extremists. It became very important to silence the extremists on behalf of the centrists.

When a vote resulted in winners and losers, I would act happy, not sad. I would then activate the centrists to create compromises and directions that appealed more to them than to the extremists. This was new behavior for me because I really did worry about the losers. They were hurt. They were excluded. They might take their marbles and go home. But the more I worried about their hurt and their marbles, the more I fed their extremism. Thus, learning to love the vote has been a positive breakthrough. I have withdrawn oxygen from the extremists; their fires burn less brightly.

More Space, Less Anxiety

Second, I have learned how important it is to create voting situations that are smart. Not "this congregation opposes the war in Iraq" so much as "the members of the Just Peace group oppose the war in Iraq and are taking signatures from the membership after the service today." When unity of the whole is impossible, creating space for actions that do not involve the whole can be very important.

The third way I changed my behavior was to learn the strange art of self-differentiation. Self-differentiation is what Ed Friedman, the late guru of congregational studies, advised for clergy when he spoke of a "non-anxious presence." I always had too deep a mother-hen streak to do that well. My art was inclusion and presence. I thought that not to show a little anxiety meant not to care.

I never experienced much anxiety at all in ministry until I ran into genuine diversity of opinion under one roof. Being anxious about this diversity was indeed my original modus operandi. Now I am teaching myself how not to be anxious about something that has very little to do with me. I am still drawn into triangulation over the issues, but most of the issues we face are between members, each of whom want me on their side. Staying out of the middle is now my favorite dance step.

Hospitality for Some

Fourth, I have begun to express genuine disapproval for extremists who care more about their own opinions, culture, or tastes than about their fellow members. And I am letting go of those who can't "share." This fourth behavior has been very difficult. I have always assumed that if a member leaves a church it means I did something wrong.

I know that isn't logical. I know that the boundaries in that kind of thinking are badly drawn. But I still feel that it is my job to get my arms around the whole parish and to make the sacred space safe and comfortable for them. I see that as my call. They are the members; it is their church. I am not without responsibilities regarding hospitality, especially the creation of a hospitable place. Developing disrespect for extremists and antagonists has involved traveling a long road. Once wanting hospitality for all, I have come to be satisfied with hospitality for some.

Sticking to Our Core

Fifth, I have found that prayer—accessing God—is the best way to avoid triangulation. God is never found on one side or another of these wickedly silly debates. That is important for me and important for the parish to know. Prayer accomplishes the delivery of that message. We can act without consensus in the name of our majority's best understanding of what God wants.

Sixth, when I do get free of negative reactions and postures, I do best to spend my time focusing on issues of core values. Because the parish includes extremes of both liberal and conservative, both open and closed people, I have had to be careful to take care of the center. The two edges each contain about 10 percent of the people. That means that the other 80 percent are in the center. Focusing on them, rather than the loud, demanding edges, helps the congregation stick to its core. There remain some things on which we all agree, and we head for them every proactive minute we get.

Diversity Is Not Easy

Seventh, I have come to more deeply appreciate and accept the very diversity that has caused all this pain. Over the years, I have found it easy to be a pastor to people with whom I do not agree. Some of my best friends are Republicans. Currently, though, the culture wars are so extreme that I can't reach to my "other" side without being suspect. There is something very strained now in this parish; stretching my kind of arm all the way around it is not as easy as it was 10 years ago. The culture wars are increasing in decibel level. Ironically, the genuine diversity we have achieved makes hospitality, and therefore governance, very hard.

I have to remind myself often that this country elected our president in a nearly tied election. That election fell apart in Miami, Dade County, where I minister. The diversity of opinion about where to lead the country is real. It is also the context in which I work. Consensus will not always be possible. Having winners and losers is not the ideal situation. So we must vote, and simply take turns winning and losing. Absent consensus, that becomes my objective—to rotate the losses and victories so that no one constituency starts to own everything.

In Search of Balance

Eighth and finally, I spend much time teaching people about themselves. Some will not realize that moving the choir (which has now grown to 59 voices) to the front of the sanctuary will be disruptive.

Some want their worship just the way it has always been, whether or not the choir explodes out of the choir loft. Does that mean we shouldn't make changes? Of course not. But we need to balance these changes. When the choir loft people "win," there needs to be a "win" for the sacred stability crowd who really do feel threatened when a new hymn or hymnal or liturgical practice shows up. This is especially true when the two sides are close to being equal in numbers. When we took a straw vote one Sunday, 151 people wanted the choir in the front and 140 wanted it in the back.

For my own mental health, I have had to learn not to care so much about these squabbles. For the sake of the gospel and my call to serve it, I have had to learn to be cunningly hospitable, on a rotating basis. For the sake of the diversity that I do believe is part of God's reign, I have had to abandon consensus.

Learning to Pastor a Small Congregation

ANDREW D. HAGEN

"Whoever is faithful in a very little is faithful also in much."
(Luke 16:10)

Nothing prepared me for the experience of pastoring the small congregation to which I was first called. Neither my personal experience nor my seminary training had any relation to the dynamics, needs, goals, concerns, or style of ministry found in a smaller congregation. What is worse, I entered believing that there must be something wrong with churches that remain small. It is only by God's grace and years of struggling that I survived such poor preparation and such a bad attitude. It took several years of floundering around before I realized that the biggest problem this smaller church had was not its size, but its pastor.

Let me cite a few embarrassing examples. The first involved leadership. Since this was a smaller church, I assumed the role of the pastor would carry with it a great amount of power and authority. This is true and also very false. It is true that you can do just about anything you want to as the pastor of a small church: you can start Bible studies, support groups, and community service programs at will. You can do these things—but don't expect anyone to join in. The pastor may have the power to initiate a program but the people have the power to vote with their feet. I soon discovered that pastor-initiated programs, even

---

Originally published in *Congregations,* vol. 24, no. 1 (January/February 1998), pp. 14–15.

excellent ones, did not stand a chance unless there were two or three members on board as well. This might also be true in a larger church, but the results might be less noticeable.

The second example has to do with the way ministry is carried out in a smaller congregation. I entered this setting believing that ministry was done only through programs and committees. Since I was concerned about the growth of this smaller church, I used all my experience and education to come to the brilliant conclusion that we needed to start an evangelism committee. I gathered together the few who were willing to serve, we studied our dire need to grow, and then we became discouraged and quietly fell apart in less than a year.

The final example concerns pastoral care. I believed that pastoral care was best accomplished in pastoral counseling. Whenever an individual seemed troubled or when a problem arose, I urged him or her to come see me for an hour in my office. This is how I could best show my pastoral concern in time of need, I thought. I was disappointed that very few people responded. As a result I logged very few hours of pastoral counseling and felt quite discouraged.

Sometime in my third year as pastor I began to realize that I really didn't understand how to serve this smaller congregation effectively. Few things were getting accomplished and no one had yet commissioned a portrait of me in honor of my faithful service. I began to understand; the problem was that I was trying to pastor a smaller church as if it were a much bigger one. I realized that my ministry to this congregation would not be successful until I began to pay attention to the unique dynamics of its size. This revelation gave me a sense of rebirth and excitement as I saw the challenge ahead.

A New Metaphor

I realized that I needed to develop a new metaphor for my role as pastor. If this church were a ship, my role as pastor was not to have a hand on the tiller steering its course but rather a seat in the crow's nest looking for the dangers and opportunities ahead. Since pastoral turnover in smaller churches is relatively frequent, the congregation is legitimately concerned about pastors who set the course and then abandon ship. But they truly value the education and vision of their pastors and rely upon them to prevent them from looking only to the past. So I climbed into the crow's nest and happily provided that kind of leadership with much support and success.

In the area of ministry, I realized it should be focused more on people than on programs. Because of our size, we could not carry out many complicated programs. But I learned that certain people were willing to take responsibility for specific ministries. It didn't take a committee to deliver the collection to the food pantry—it took an older couple with a few spare hours a month. The property committee didn't plant the flowers—one man with a green thumb came by and did that. One family sets up the Christmas tree every year and four or five friends gather to plan the annual picnic. My role was not to organize or direct, but rather to be a resource, a supporter, and most importantly, to lend a hand. When I was tempted to start a new "program," I made sure that I had at least one person who was willing to take responsibility for it. I still struggle with my programmatic orientation, but I've learned not to argue with the successful style of a smaller church.

I also made changes in terms of pastoral care. Perhaps in some churches pastoral care includes formal counseling, but in a smaller church it is less obvious or measurable. Sometimes care is shown simply at the back of the sanctuary when one remembers to ask about a member's grandson who broke his leg. It may mean using a person's name when distributing communion or sending someone's daughter a note when she makes the honor roll. I found that a simple, personal birthday card to each member communicated more pastoral care than any other effort I had made. And when times got really tough, I learned to go to people's homes, not have them come to my office. The joy of a smaller church is that pastoral care can be shown to everyone all the time in ways not possible in larger congregations.

My whole attitude about pastoring a smaller congregation changed. I collected a library of resources that weren't available at the seminary bookstore. My members were pleased that they trained me right—even if it took five years. And something else amazing happened. We began to grow! It makes sense that when the ministry and the context start to match, a sense of excitement and health develops. This good feeling is infectious among the members and magnetic to outsiders. However, we then developed a new problem: adjusting to being a smaller church getting bigger! I guess that is what Jesus meant when he said, "Whoever is faithful in a very little is faithful also in much."

Leadership in a Non-Staff-Dependent Congregation

BILL JONES

There are many helpful ways of classifying congregations: by size (small, medium, large); by how churches "work" (matriarchal/ patriarchal, pastoral, program-centered, or corporate model); by theological inclination (liberal, conservative, middle-of-the-road); by geography or history ("we used to be downtown, but moved to the suburbs," "that church chews up a minister every five years").

A few years ago, I moved from one church to another expecting the two congregations to be very similar. Both were middle-sized, with many young families and a healthy population of children and youth. Both churches valued music, worshipped informally, and generally supported their denomination. Both were located in areas of potential growth.

But, after making the move, I discovered one way in which the two congregations were significantly different. I had moved to a church that was consciously not staff-dependent from one that had probably never thought about it one way or the other. I found myself having to learn new styles of ministry and leadership and asking myself some questions that seemed very important.

How does a congregation come to see itself as not dependent on staff? What do we ministers and other church professionals do to promote or discourage this development in a congregation? What kind of leadership is needed for the laity to want to claim responsibility for the life and ministry of a church?

Originally published in *Congregations*, vol. 22, no. 6 (November/December 1996), pp. 6–9.

My own reflections on these questions are very preliminary; I am still learning. It has been helpful to me to look back on where I have been, to look closely at where I am now, and to bring theological reflection to this journey. The issue of staff dependency is not unconnected to our understanding of what a church is in the first place. I share these preliminary reflections with the hope that they will lead to broader discussion among people who care about the church.

What Is a Staff-Dependent Church Like?

It is important for me to recognize that I have not moved from a "bad" church to a "good" church. The fact is, both are good congregations, with their fair share of typical—and not so typical—problems.

I spent eleven years in a very positive pastoral relationship with a congregation of energetic, friendly people who were busy both in and outside the church. The congregation attracted a steady stream of new members over the years. It had vital Christian education, fellowship opportunities, and mission and outreach programs. Most of the years, the treasurer reported there was a little money in the bank.

But my memories of those years include a time in which I came very close to burnout. I reached a point where I felt a deep weariness and hopelessness about the future.

Since that time, a light has turned on for me about my experience. I realize I am working at least as hard now as I was then, even harder in some ways, but I am feeling nothing of the burnout I felt then. The difference has to do with responsibility.

I believe I carried the burden of an inappropriate sense of responsibility for that church. My vision of what the church should be to that congregation drove me in my ministry. The trouble was, the congregation did not seem to own my vision. It did not drive them. (Nor did I ask them about their vision of what a church should be.)

Basically, my vision had to do with creating a community of faith that was the central community in the lives of its members, the community that defined who they were and what they did with all of their lives. One person cannot create a community, no matter how hard he or she works at it! The congregation responded well to my preaching, teaching, and leadership (at least on the whole; over the years, those who did not respond dropped out or moved on). But, as the years passed, I noticed that I was initiating most of the programs. For example, I initiated a youth program that worked as long as I was in charge, but floundered when I tried to pass it on to the laity.

This became a frustrating pattern. At one point, I developed a policy statement for the session in which my own responsibilities and those of the elders were clearly spelled out. The discussion was positive. The statement was clear, well-written, and unanimously adopted. But nothing changed. I now realize that things did not change because it was my policy. It addressed my problem.

I can see now that one way we functioned in a staff-dependent way was through my feeling of responsibility as moderator of the session. I believed it was my job to see that the elders arrived at consensus before any vote was taken. I had to understand how every issue should turn out and how to get to a peaceful consensus. I felt responsible for protecting the leadership of the church from conflict!

The members of the church were typically busy, but being busy is not the same thing as being responsible. It was clearly the responsibility of the "professionals" (who know more about such things) to worry about whether or not our church school program was actually accomplishing what we wanted; the congregation was doing its part by showing up.

People cared about the church. When they brought their concerns to the staff, the implication was, "We care enough to tell the person in charge."

About the time of my worst burnout I heard the joke about the small-town minister who had the strange habit of stopping whatever he was doing and rushing to the train station every day to watch the 11:45 express go through town. People who observed this were puzzled. The train didn't stop so he couldn't be meeting anyone. Why did he do it? Finally someone mustered the courage to ask the minister, who answered that he liked to watch the train go through because it was the only thing in that town that moved without his pushing it.

I know the feeling.

People in dependent relationships have a million ways of maintaining that dependency. "We are so thankful you are here." "We just know a bigger church is going to take you away." "You are the only reason I go to this church." I can now see the unhealthiness of these statements. I can also see some of the ways a so-called responsible person has of protecting others from the burden of bearing some of that responsibility. "I know how busy you are; I'll do that for you."

What Is a Non-Staff-Dependent Congregation Like?

Just as a congregation that has never asked itself questions about staff dependency is not necessarily "bad," a church that has embraced the decision not to be staff dependent is not thereby "good."

Early in my move to a new congregation, I began to have some disorienting experiences.

I would arrive at church in the evening for a meeting and discover another meeting taking place that I did not know about. Why didn't I know about that meeting? Did it mean I was not sufficiently on top of things? Was there some reason those people did not want me at their meeting? Should I be concerned? Or pleased?

I made some inquiries and was told that the minister is not expected to attend every meeting and that when I was needed I would surely be invited! (Message: let us be responsible.)

The point at which that first family asks to join the church after a new minister arrives is a time of great joy and relief for the new minister. It also turned out to be an occasion of continuing education!

I shared our "good news" with an elder and suggested we call a session meeting to receive new members between church school and worship the next Sunday. The quorum for receiving new members is small and should only take about five minutes.

The elder did not know me very well yet, but had enough gumption to say that, ordinarily in this congregation, new members go through inquirer's class before they join and that the session meeting is important enough not to rush.

I am convinced that such a conversation never would have happened at my former church. Here was the laity explaining to me that the process into membership in the congregation is important and it matters how well it is done!

Of course, when we move into new leadership situations, we bring old leadership styles with us. What else have we to bring? I received rave reviews on my moderating of session meetings...at first. Meetings moved along decently and in order. I paid attention to agendas and had a knack for helping the session through sticky issues.

But after a year or two, I began to hear some grumbling: elders said they felt unnecessary at meetings; that nothing significant happened; and that they did not really feel they were being called on to lead.

These people helped me examine and change my understanding of the moderator's role. The moderator's job is to be sure that issues are clear, that questions are answered, that the playing field is level, and that all sides will be heard. Sometimes a moderator's job is to remind people to say what they think in the meeting, not in the parking lot after the meeting, and to articulate the larger vision ("Remember who we are; it's fine to disagree, even passionately, but after the vote is taken, we still love each other!")

When laity give themselves permission to argue, disagree, pray together, laugh and cry together in a setting where they know they will be loved after the vote is taken, responsibility is taken for the church being the church. The laity become responsible for the decisions made and the consequences of the decisions.

I have learned to recognize many of the ways this congregation chooses to perpetuate its decision not to be staff dependent.

When someone visits this church for the first time, they are greeted by the laity, not the staff. When they become interested in joining the church, they are invited to an inquirer's class that is led by the laity. At the session meeting where they are received, every elder takes time to talk about what the church has meant to her or him and to offer specific invitations for ways the new member can get involved. ("If you are interested, speak to me"—not the pastor!) They are introduced in worship by lay people.

Almost every time we worship, there is a lay person participating in the leadership. We are exploring ways to train the laity to do this better, but flawless is not our goal in worship. The congregation sees this as affirmation that worship belongs to us, not to the professionals.

All of the committees of session meet at the same time once a month. The staff can only be available for resource and support; we cannot be responsible for the work of the committees. And even the session's agenda is produced at a meeting of the committee chairs with the pastor and clerk of session.

One of the essential questions I have had to ask myself these last few years is: What kind of leadership is needed in a congregation that chooses not to be staff dependent? I am still working at answering that question for myself in this congregation. The answer has to do with things like providing leadership training, support and nurture, and visioning.

Does This Really Matter? (Theological Reflections)

I do not want to tack on a few theological reflections at the end of these thoughts as if to give them weight. I hope it is already clear that the issue of staff dependency is essential to an understanding of what a church is.

But the need to do some specific theological reflection seems crucial today in light of much of what I read about church growth and what congregations need to do to reach baby boomers, for instance.

Much of what I read seems to be based on the assumption that there are some crucial problems facing the church that professional church people must address. We talk about baby boomers as if they were people we must attract into our congregations at all costs. I see little being written about what the church becomes if the members are attracted for one reason or another into communities for which they sense no responsibility.

We are not called to be growth institutions or even smooth-running organizations. We are called to be the body of Christ in the world. We are called to do ministry. We are called to form communities that are shaped by the word and spirit of God. And this calling holds the promise of transforming us into new creations.

No staff person can make any of this happen, no matter how much skill or energy is brought to the job. I am discovering that where the laity own responsibility for the life and ministry of the community of faith, people want to be equipped and empowered and enjoy telling others that the church is changing their lives.

There is of course always the danger that a congregation may have a radically different vision of how it should "be the church in that place" than the minister and staff. Bad matches occur. But the assumption that such vision resides exclusively in professional staff is a contradiction of our theology. We say that Christ is the head of the church and that the church is the body of Christ. It is the work of each congregation to grow and struggle toward an understanding of its vision and ministry. Where this is owned as a congregational responsibility, I am discovering that the laity is empowered and the staff is energized.

Is your congregation dependent on the staff?

- Who in your congregation calls and schedules committee meetings?
- Who prepares the agenda for committee meetings?
- If the pastor moderates the session or vestry, who else participates in the preparation of the agenda?
- Who is responsible for following up on business approved in committees to see that it is carried out?
- A part of the issue of staff dependency is "who thinks for the congregation?" (This is like the designated parent whose job it is to make sure everyone in the family is doing his or her chores.) Is there someone in your congregation who functions, formally or informally, in this role?
- The question of staff dependency raises certain issues that are better discussed than answered in a questionnaire:

    a. How protective is your staff of its control?
    b. What do you perceive as the dangers and benefits of developing real lay leadership in congregations?

When Women Lead the Flock

ANN SVENNUNGSEN

For over 30 years I have thought about the pioneering role of women as leaders. It began in 1972 when I lost to a boy in the vote for student body president of my high school in Shelby, Montana. It continued when I successfully won a similar election in college, becoming the first woman student association president in the school's 85-year history. Then, for 22 years, I served as a pastoral leader. In each congregation, I had a pioneering role: the first woman *pastor,* the first woman *co-pastor,* the first woman *senior pastor.*

What difference did it make that I was a woman? Do women lead differently from men? Are girls socialized to lead in certain ways? How do women incorporate what is good for leadership from their socialization, and how do they overcome what is bad? There are several studies on women in ministry, such as those described in the Pulpit & Pew report "Women's Path into Ministry: Six Major Studies." These studies compare the ministry styles of men and women in various areas: preaching, presiding at worship, teaching, pastoral care, placement, and loneliness.

My focus is on women as pastoral *leaders.* Leadership is a timely topic in both church and society. Not long ago, my alma mater changed its mission statement to read "Luther Seminary educates *leaders* for Christian communities" [emphasis added], and the *New York Times* regularly includes books about leadership on its bestseller list. In my

Originally published in *Congregations,* vol. 30, no. 3 (Summer 2004), pp. 21–24.

work as a woman in pastoral leadership, two such books have been particularly significant: *Primal Leadership: Realizing the Power of Emotional Intelligence* by Daniel Goleman, Annie McKee, and Richard Boyatzis; and *Leadership without Easy Answers* by Ronald Heifetz.

Leadership and Emotional Intelligence

In *Primal Leadership,* the authors focus on emotional intelligence, arguing that "the best leaders have found effective ways to understand and improve the way they handle their own and other people's emotions. . . .This emotional task of the leader is primal . . . in two senses: It is both the original and the most important act of leadership."[1] The book suggests 18 competencies of emotional intelligence, including emotional self-awareness, emotional self-control, empathy, and relationship management. Throughout the book, I was struck by a sense that women and girls were socialized to do just what the authors were asking—to pay close attention to emotions and to relationships. I often caught myself thinking, "Well, duh, of course you need empathy and relational skills to lead!" This is not big news for a woman.

Indeed, as I reflect on my leadership style, these intelligences are some of the best gifts I bring. When critical decision-making is needed, my first step is to gather people together, bringing wisdom and ownership to the table. When a change is suggested "on the fly," I take time to ensure that other stakeholders are consulted. Occasionally, this attention to relationships has been frustrating to those who wish to move with greater expediency. However, in the long run, it has served the organization well. There is a deeper sense of trust within the group—a confidence that each participant will be respected and included—and a belief that better decisions will result from attention to process.

However, attention to relationships can sometimes become an impediment for leadership. In her book *Odd Girl Out,* Rachel Simmons studies the development of girls ages 10 to 14. She notes earlier studies that discovered that, while boys fear smothering, girls fear isolation.[2] This socialization affects adulthood roles, as Simmons notes in her reference to CNN Executive Vice President Gall Evans' book, *Play Like a Man, Win Like a Woman:*

After decades of watching women hit the glass ceiling, Evans concludes that a misguided focus on personal relationships is partly to
blame.... Women struggle when hearing the word no from colleagues
or superiors, construing it as a sign of interpersonal conflict. Because
of this, women will avoid asking questions they anticipate will end in
a no, hearing it as 'a sign the relationship between us and our superiors has failed.' . . . Where Evans has watched men buy each other a
beer after a conflict at work, a woman often takes it personally. She
may storm away angry, reflecting a lifetime association of conflict
with relational loss. Women who, as girls, never learned to be comfortable with conflict now as adults have trouble distinguishing normal day-to-day disagreements from personal attacks.[3]

I recall such an experience from my tenth year of ministry. To high-
light our annual stewardship program, I suggested that each council
committee prepare a brief dramatic presentation to present between
worship services. The idea was quickly and soundly rejected. As one
lay leader said, "Unlike you, Ann, most of us would be pretty uncom-
fortable at the thought of doing some sort of Bible camp skit." I was
devastated—embarrassed for even suggesting such an idea. I came home
with a sense of personal rejection, and it took a while before I felt con-
fident enough to offer another creative idea.

By my twentieth year of ministry, I had become more comfortable
with the leader's vocation of suggesting ideas and casting vision. When
my congregation considered a new program for Wednesday worship
and education, I brought a rough proposal to the staff. By the end of
the meeting, the final proposal looked nothing like my original, but I
was not embarrassed. I did not feel rejected. I had come to see that the
leader's vocation includes casting the initial vision—setting forth ideas
that will be changed and improved through a process of critique and
discussion. Indeed, when I think back to that stewardship program several years earlier, I realize that the final outcome was actually shaped by
my original idea—the one that was soundly rejected. It has been significant to recognize that the leader's vocation includes casting a vision, making initial proposals, and knowing that corporate critique and
improvement is not sign of rejection but rather a cause for celebration.

Yes, though women may be well equipped for empathy and relationship management, these strengths may also become stumbling blocks. Clearly there is a tension—attention to relationships on the one hand and self-differentiation on the other. And, perhaps, gender socialization has something to say about the side of the horse off which one is apt to fall. In the words of feminist theologian Daphne Hampson, of Scotland's St. Andrews University, "The task for men is . . . to learn to find themselves *in relationship;* the task for women is to find *themselves* in relationship."[4]

Leadership and Authority

Just as gender socialization affects a leader's development with respect to Goleman's key emotional intelligences of empathy and relationship management, so also gender socialization plays a role in the relationship between leadership and authority.

At a recent gathering of seasoned pastors, there was consensus that pastoral authority is both granted and earned, and that gender plays a role in the relationship and balance between the two.

In his book *Leadership without Easy Answers,* Ronald Heifetz defines authority as "conferred power to perform a service"—"Given your know-how, I give you the power to make decisions to accomplish a service, and I'll follow those decisions as long as it appears to me that they serve my purposes." He continues with this caveat: "Not all authority relationships are the product of a conscious and deliberate conferring of power. Often, they are produced by habitual deference."[5]

One might argue that men come into the pastoral office with greater external authority as a result of "habitual deference" to clergy—who have been consistently male. Such authority is not immediately conferred upon women, who do not "look like" the clergy to whom deference was given in the past. There is a greater need to earn authority— authority conferred once a parishioner comes to learn that the woman pastor has the know-how, the wisdom, and the gifts to provide the service the parishioner expects.

As a Lutheran, my first pastoral assignment was a year of internship, serving full-time as "student pastor." Eager for the experience, I was deeply troubled to learn that the seminary placement office received two rejections before finding me an assignment. I had excellent grades, good recommendations—all was in order, except that it was 1979 and I was a woman.

Such experiences of rejection slowed the development of my inner authority. I thought to myself, "If all those Christians are unwilling to consider me as their pastor, what actually gives me the authority to minister?" Even when I could intellectually debunk such thinking, the feelings remained. It is not surprising that women struggle to establish a strong sense of inner authority.

In her article "Weaving Garments of Grace: En-gendering a Theology of the Call to Ordained Ministry for Women Today," Joy McDougall also discovers the truth of this. In her conversation with eight gifted women seminary students, she tells how they expressed frustration with external impediments to ordination. But, what "stunned" the author was the women's "self-doubts, ambivalence, and even guilt about (their) call to ordained ministry: 'Did I really want to set myself apart within my church community?' 'I was petrified about standing in the pulpit for the first time to preach. I didn't think I could do it.' 'I think I felt guilty about wanting to be a priest, as if I thought that I was somehow better than others or spiritually elite.'"[6]

Leadership and Improvisation

In addition to the relationship between leadership and authority, Heifetz suggests that leadership requires a willingness to improvise: "Leadership...requires an experimental mindset, the willingness to work by trial and error—where the community's reactions at each stage provide the basis for planning future actions."[7] Pastors practice that improvisation in the context of a very complex community—replete with a host of different constituencies—lay and pastoral staff, elected leaders, appointed leaders, self-appointed leaders, and so on.

Clearly, in such a complex community, issues of gender will play a part in the leader's work of improvisation. The community's reactions may and will be influenced by the leader's gender. Both women *and* men need to acknowledge and understand this. However, women may need to be especially aware. In my most recent call as senior pastor of a 3,700-member congregation, I occasionally would suggest that conflicts I encountered might be based, in part, on gender. One day, the male council president looked at me and said, "Why do you bring up the gender thing?" I was reminded of my work in race relations—where, if you are a person of color, race is *always* an issue. In the same way, if you are a woman working in patriarchal culture, gender is *always* an issue.

However, gender is not always *the* issue. Actually, one of the challenges facing women leaders is the need to discern the cause of a particular struggle. On the one hand, we ourselves are sometimes the cause—our personality, our ministry style, a mistake we've made. On the other hand, struggles sometimes arise from within the congregation—dysfunctional lay leadership, an unresolved issue in the congregation's history, staff conflict. However, for women in pioneering roles, there is also a third possibility—the issue of gender. We find ourselves asking, "Is this struggle in any way related to the fact that I am a woman in leadership?"

Clearly, one has to be careful about raising the gender question. There are essentially two pitfalls: raising the gender question too often and failing to raise the question at all. To blame every problem on sexism is to deny reality and inhibit one's own personal growth as a woman in leadership. On the other hand, to deny that sexism potentially could be a factor is also to deny reality. Still, the subtleties for this discernment can be enormous.

Occasionally, I have had the experience of suggesting an idea to which no one takes notice. Some moments later, however, a man makes a similar suggestion, and the whole room responds. Then, one must ask, "Is this a function of group process, where an idea becomes more favorable as the discussion continues, or is this an issue of gender discrimination, whereby an idea expressed by a man is given more credibility than the same idea expressed by a woman?" Clearly there are many layers. The work of leading a congregation is always an adventure with myriad dynamics, some of which are neither fair nor just. Still, that is the real world in which we are called to serve.

Leadership and Faith

Yes, the relationship between gender socialization and leadership development is complicated. And sometimes, like my friends who resist the Myers-Briggs test because they do not want their multifaceted personalities reduced to a list of four mere letters, so I also resist being reduced to a particular leadership style because I am a woman. We are much more than our gender. Nevertheless, there is important learning to be gained through the appropriate study of these issues.

Indeed, some wonder why the issue is not being studied more fully. "Why is the issue of gender largely absent from contemporary discussions about the crisis of pastoral leadership? This seems especially surprising, since most sociologists and theological educators agree that women's entry into the ordained ministry represents the most significant transformation in pastoral leadership in the twentieth century, if not since the Reformation."[8] Yes, faithful and honest conversation about women in pastoral leadership is important. Through study and awareness, growth and change, the church can become better equipped to lead and to serve in faithfulness. There are important strides to be made and a great deal to explore as we move toward a roster of pastors that better reflects the rich diversity of God's people.

One of the best stories from my ministry comes from a four-year-old parishioner, Elizabeth. Though Erik Strand and I had been her pastors since she was baptized as an infant, I had just announced that I was leaving the congregation and moving to Iowa. Sometime after she heard the news, she turned to her mother and said, "Mommy, isn't it sad that God is moving to Iowa? But," she said, "at least Jesus is staying here."

Though her theology was a bit suspect, Elizabeth pointed to the best leadership example: Follow Jesus. Seek the ways of God. Pray hard. And most important, lead and live by grace.

Notes

1. Daniel Goleman, Annie McKee, and Richard Boyatzis. *Primal Leadership: Realizing the Power of Emotional Intelligence* (Boston: Harvard Business School Press, 2002): 4–5.

2. Rachel Simmons, *Odd Girl Out: The Hidden Culture of Aggression in Girls* (Orlando, Fla.: Harcourt, 2002): 30.
3. Ibid., 265–266.
4. Daphne Hampson, "Reinhold Niebuhr on Sin: A critique" in Richard Harries, ed., *Reinhold Niebuhr and the Issues of Our Time* (Grand Rapids, Mich.: Eerdmans, 1986): 55.
5. Ronald Heifetz, *Leadership without Easy Answers* (Cambridge, Mass.: Belknap Press of Harvard University Press, 1998): 57–58.
6. Joy McDougall, "Weaving Garments of Grace: En-gendering a Theology of the Call to Ordained Ministry for Women Today," *Theological Education*, Vol. 39, No. 2 (Pittsburgh, Pa.: The Association of Theological Schools in the United States and Canada, 2003): 150.
7. Heifetz, 242.
8. McDougall, 151.

Forming God's People

MARK LAU BRANSON

A few years ago, I asked a group of pastors to list the obligations and roles specified in our legislated denominational materials. As I listed these duties on a screen, the murmuring began. As leader of this retreat, I was supposed to provide a moderate dose of clarity and encouragement for colleagues who had asked for help with burnout, a dearth of collegial relationships, and little agreement on what we as clergy were hoping to accomplish. It was obvious that this exercise did not encourage the group. More than three dozen separate items were included, and over 50 verbs. "Supervise ... administer ... care ... report ... preach ... cooperate ... evaluate ... search ... counsel ... lead ... oversee ... prepare ... provide ... deploy ... obtain ... maintain ... " Our documents specified topics for counseling, contexts for ministry, and, of course, denominational duties. The murmuring continued; then the pastors began laughing. They sat right there, in the presence of a judicatory leader who had a supervisory role, and they laughed at the job description.

When we look for resources to guide our modes of leadership, we are provided with a smorgasbord of types and metaphors. Consumer choice reigns, and pastors are tempted to deliver on the images. You might be a type-A CEO who creates and manages a "tall-steeple church" or a "megachurch." You may prefer being an activist in the Saul Alinsky mold to help us act (or feel) really liberal (or conservative). Your style

Originally published in *Congregations,* vol. 29, no. 1 (Winter 1995): pp. 23–27.

may be that of a motivational speaker who can intensify our spiritual affections.

Those who promote each image give us reasons that suit our desires for organizational successes, along with no small nod to our internal insecurities and drives. We might seek a pastor who serves as alter ego, as therapist, or as a parent who accepts or scolds or serves as a target for some leftover antiauthoritarian arrows. We may want a shepherd to be an all-sufficient guide, provider, and rescuer. Perhaps a teacher-sage would assure us that we are thoughtful and educated, then leave us to be enlightened adults who make up our own minds. If our priority is preserving a traditional institution and its financial holdings, we need a manager-controller. And even though we will use other terms, we may desire an entertainer whose sermons are at least marginally competitive with sports or concerts or, more likely, the lure of a latte with the Sunday paper.

Leading Where and Why

It is critical that leadership be understood as a secondary question. The prior work concerns ecclesiology, soteriology, and missiology—or what we mean by church, salvation, and mission. Through our leadership, what do we wish to create or move or form or produce? I hear church leaders who hope to lead massive growth, or institutional survival, or civic engagement. But we need to ask: Growth of *what*? Survival of *what*? *What* engagement, and *why*? Congregational leaders need constantly to ask: What is the church? And what is the church in this place? In *Models of the Church*, Avery Dulles—priest, professor, and now cardinal—gave us a useful set of images. Each model could be used to develop appropriate dimensions to our leadership: institutions need managers, heralds articulate a message, servants express compassion and mercy. It is notable that Dulles's revised edition features a new model, "community of disciples," which he develops as a synthesizing and inclusive type.

Dulles's attention to "community" counters rampant individualism as well as cultural definitions of community that include little more than affinity and affection. Dulles draws attention to specific qualities that seldom merit focus in many U.S. churches: relative intimacy, permanence, and proximity.[1] These characteristics counter the congregational models that acquiesce to our society's norms. We tend toward casual relationships (we've lost the long evenings of storytelling, and we seldom interfere in each others' lives). We live commuter lives (work, friends, recreation, school, church). And we relocate frequently (for reasons of career and taste). If our congregations want to realize the traits Dulles notes, we will need to give adequate attention to geography, more significant time together, and committed covenant practices. Only with these emphases can a congregation promote consistency in discipleship and meaningful engagement with a neighborhood. In *The Problem of Christianity* Josiah Royce emphasized a community's need for shared memories, cooperative activities (what sociologist Robert Bellah has called "committed practices"), and common hopes.[2]

Converging social forces have successfully embedded an imagined "good life" in our psyche and social formation—a salvation story that leads to habits of consumerism, careerism, and many levels of sanctioned and unsanctioned violence. Churches and pastors often serve as chaplains to this national project, perhaps offering moderating voices but generally keeping faith and church circumscribed to minimal practices. Akin to other civic players, church leaders find our niche (providing animated or staid worship, a food bank, a religious comment in civic settings). Clergy's place is dictated by society, church is tagged onto the numerous commitments of all the members, and our relationships and imaginations are centered elsewhere.

What are we leaders to do if we take these descriptors of community seriously? How would one lead such a community if it is to display a thorough and distinctive association with Jesus? What memories need to be owned and repeated as common memories? How do we define "hope?" How might worship and love and ethics and jobs cohere? What cooperative activities are essential? How do we define and encourage proximity and permanence? What countering forces should we expect?

Giving Structure to a Vision

In an urban United Methodist church, a few families wanted to reenvision how our lives embodied our faith. We were several years into Bible study, social analysis, covenant groups, mission attempts, and continuing growth as a multicultural congregation. Some biblical passages had lured us—Jeremiah called for immigrant Hebrews (actually interned war prisoners) to envision several generations of life and service in Babylon (Jer. 29). Isaiah's imaginative poetry celebrated a visible urban community that attracted the commendation and participation of others (Isa. 58). Luke's accounts in Acts and Paul's priorities in his letters gave us a sustained look at the Holy Spirit's generative and corrective work of establishing identifiably covenanted communities.

These studies, and our analysis of urban forces, plus hours of prayer and stories, had led us to consider creating a cohousing[3] community. Biblical images gave us the meanings we needed; continuing hours of conversation and labor built our relationships; planning and budgeting and delegating inched us forward to carry out this corporate project. Themes of community, ecology, and neighbors gave structure to our vision. We built and remodeled nine units, for various family sizes, with organic gardens, solar power, frequent meals with each other and with guests, and commitments to the neighborhood. Our church practices of plural leadership were evident in the shared work of envisioning, laboring, and caring about relationships.

This project illustrates how leadership needs to function in a congregation. *Interpretive leadership* creates and provides resources for a community of interpreters who pay attention to God, texts, context, and congregation. *Relational leadership* creates and nourishes all of the human connections in various groups, partnerships, friendships, and families. *Implemental leadership* develops strategies and structures so that a congregation embodies gospel reconciliation and justice in a local context and in the larger world. In effect, these three spheres are structures in the congregations—structures that give meanings (interpretive), human connections (relational), and organizational practices (implemental). It is crucial that a congregation's primary leaders nurture capacities and skills in all three spheres, and that they are attentive to cohesive and coherent practices in the context of constant change.

Interpretive Leadership

Interpretive leadership creates a learning community. A community of interpreters uses the available literary, social, and spiritual skills to give attention to "texts" while listening to and observing God's initiatives. The texts of Scripture and tradition require more at-

tention than a Sunday sermon; those who are being formed into a covenant community will give considerable time and energy to study. The
scriptural metanarrative[4] and the individual writers and their narratives require significant attention. What do we mean by "covenant" or
"gospel" or "faithful"? What does it mean to be a "church"? How did
our faith ancestors worship? What kind of faith communities did they
form? How were they to relate to neighbors? What mission is God's
mission?

Further, the congregation's life, its history, and its makeup need
attention. Various venues can be formed for the telling of *spiritual* autobiographies. I have also seen the benefits of telling *cultural* autobiographies and *money* autobiographies. The congregation as a whole also
has a story. The official narratives give too much attention to clergy
and buildings; we need to uncover stories of faith, of mission, of spiritual strength, and of woundedness. In the Japanese-American Presbyterian church where my family has become active, we have created
numerous conversations with "appreciative inquiry" interviews. This
approach surfaces the strongest and most life-giving stories and characteristics of an organization. The congregation is gaining the capacity
to see a more hopeful future that is generated by the best of its past.
Members are becoming aware of the abundant resources for congregational reenvisioning and reinvigoration.

Leaders also equip the church to interpret the surrounding neighborhoods. The economic, social, and political stories of the city and its
neighborhoods will give perspectives on the congregation's place and
prospects. Interpretive leaders motivate storytelling and research, make
connections between congregants and neighborhoods, and build capacities for discernment. The assumption here is that logical and spiritual connections link worshiping community with the surrounding
people and powers.

Even when churches begin with organizational activities that are
well connected to gospel meanings, organizational activities and structures are often passed on without those connections. Our children in-
herit ceremonies, programs, structures, and policies that have lost their
substance. The foundational graces in Scripture, the tradition's power
and movement, are not readily available. "Meaninglessness" is not just
a subjective critique of restless youth.

Interpretive leadership provides the resources, the inspiration, the perceptions that form a people who own the biblical and historical narratives, renarrate their own personal and corporate stories, and become aware of the numerous forces that shape their context. All of these "texts" are brought to study, prayer, discernment, and envisioning as the congregation narrates and enacts its own local theology. Spirituality, then, is defined as attentiveness to and participation in the initiatives of the Holy Spirit. Church leaders create a whole congregation of interpreters as they guide and offer resources for these activities. This interpretive leadership is done with vital and deep connections to relational and implemental activities.

Relational Leadership

Numerous tip-offs announce that ours is a relational work. Covenant and salvation are essentially relational ways of being—with God, with a faith community, and with neighbor. We are to be reconciled agents of reconciliation. If meanings are to be continually discerned by the interpretive community, and if those meanings are to be made tangible and visible, the whole process will he made possible by the congregation's numerous relational connections—its groups and networks.

Within the congregation, families and friendships need leadership so that gospel meanings can be embedded and healthy relationships can be nurtured. In groups that discern, plan, and work, relational dynamics make the difference between dysfunction and banality on one hand, and lives that exhibit sanctification and justice on the other. Leaders need to be attentive to their own emotional intelligence[5] and foster that characteristic in the church. Temporary organizational movements may be based only on message and programs, but our faith calls for love.

Church leaders can renarrate and contextualize classical practices. Hospitality—a gracious offering of self and space and time—is essential for the congregation's ongoing life and for its extension to neighbors. Generosity of resources and attitudes creates dynamics that counter our society. Covenanting, paralleling the Wesleyan practices of holding "faith friends" accountable, gives opportunity for God's many gifts and graces. Belonging, often undermined by denominational norms and societal transience, is one of the most needed countercultural practices for congregational viability. Other activities like pastoral counseling and spiritual direction can be redeemed from their more individualistic forms and turned toward an attentiveness that encompasses consequences and resources for congregation and mission.

Leaders give attention and guidance and resources to this knitting together of lives. But this community formation is neither generic friendliness nor purposed on playing a prescribed role in strengthening American society. Leaders are moving from their biblically sanctified imaginations to form and equip a particular *polis*—a community whose character is thoroughly and visibly shaped by the gospel. This forming of corporate character, of vision and values and habits, takes place as the shaping powers of the society are displaced by truth as it was made visible in the Jewish carpenter's actions and teachings, and as made tangible by the Holy Spirit among us. We, as congregational leaders and participants, are redeemed from societal lies and cultural bondage as we talk and cajole and pray and forgive and cry and laugh our way to being a "city set on a hill" As we do this, we nurture a relational trust that undergirds faithful corporate life and witness.

This relational work creates the synapses, the tendons, the arteries of the body. And if leaders are forming a *polis* as they generate and orchestrate resources, then individualistic forms are converted. While our faith is profoundly personal, it is not private. Catechesis, or the initiation and instruction of those who are moving toward linking their lives with the church, is not individual discipleship but the work of making a community. Outreach is not just helping the businessperson be more ethical or the neighbor more evangelistic (although those behaviors are important). The corporate focus of New Testament metaphorical language—the word "church" or *ekklesia*, which was used to refer to gatherings for civic governance, and primary New Testament metaphors like body, city, and kingdom—emphasizes the corporate nature of our faith lives. These images have lost their distinctiveness for those of us formed by the Enlightenment, consumer choice, and the pursuit of personal careers. Relational leaders provide imagination and space for participants to be shaped as an alternative community.

Consistency is required in our interpretive leadership. Relational work, whether in pastoral counseling or in casual conversations, must not work against what the Holy Spirit is teaching the congregation in Scripture. Congregational participants (including leaders), as practicing sinners, often seek the approval of others concerning jobs, houses, expenditures, time commitments, and numerous other practices. Too often these activities come from our anxieties and fears. Our resistance to the work of Scripture and Spirit is often displayed in the common ecclesial practice of what theologian and educator Paulo Freire calls "gregariousness." We give priority to avoiding tension. We never, never, *never* want to be even remotely associated with something called a "judgment." So Bible studies offer numerous options (like a deli counter), and sermons carry the weight of editorials (maybe). Once again, being people formed as consumers, we make choice our centering characteristic. Our relational leadership must, through words and affection and touch and time and mentoring and weeping, weave something characterized by the *shalom* of justice and truth and repentance and hope that allows us to take communion and not be struck dead. That ought to be a primary goal of leaders.

Implemental Leadership

The Eucharist and other institutional practices give structural form to our meanings and relationships. Paul believed that parishioners were risking their lives and health by participating in this instituted meal when practices of truth and love were lacking. How is worship to be practiced in coherence with our meanings? In what ways does worship center our relationships and mission? Our congregations have little understanding about worship as a dangerous practice. Interpretive work needs to be a constant as we give attention to implementation.

Implemental leadership includes much of what has traditionally been considered management or administration. It is important that we form structures, develop strategies, delegate tasks, obtain and disburse resources, provide oversight, evaluate processes and results, and coach numerous other leaders. Further, leaders shape and reshape these activities amid continuous internal and external changes. These structures serve all aspects of congregational life and witness. While some things can be accomplished with total spontaneity, much of our common life requires organizational attentiveness and skills. Leaders do not have the luxury of just uttering an idea or meeting for coffee—we need to connect meanings and relationships with concrete forms and practices.

In the story above about United Methodists, some members decided to embody meanings and relationships in a cohousing community. Previously the church had taken other steps based on the formation generated in study and worship. Studies in Scripture and tradition, and honest discussion about their own lives, led many members to join covenant discipleship groups that brought accountability and encouragement to specified practices (like daily scripture reading and prayer, weekly worship and corporate Bible study, regular mission activities, and tithing). At another time the meanings of discipleship and membership were put into practice in a nine-month "exploring membership" process that allowed new members to join with greater clarity and commitment. Whenever community members are hearing the Holy Spirit's call in their lives, leaders must give attention to specific practices.

Corporate governance, missional activities integrated seamlessly with nurture and worship, facility maintenance, small-group structures, networks with other organizations, and catechesis all require careful formation and sustenance, which means implementation. A sermon well preached or relationships well cultivated or even a vision well formed can prove fruitless, lost in habitual organizational behaviors, if these three areas of leadership are not vitally connected. As leaders move among these areas of work, it is this phase of developing systems and practices that is often the center of risk, the point of courage and wonder. Seminaries offer little training, and clergy guilds tend to downplay administration as a necessary but less valuable function than preaching or counseling. But I believe it is when leadership teams, in partnership with all participants, make imaginative and costly forays into obedience that we learn what our corporate vocation is.

Praxis and Cohesion

For many years I enjoyed a collegial working friendship with the pastor of a nearby African American Presbyterian church. When we were teaching a seminary course, he once noted that his congregation was prone to act too quickly: "Our style is ready, fire, aim!" He noted that, lacking adequate attention to interpretive work, the congregation had numerous short-lived projects, and tended to wear people out. His words helped me see our church's style, which I characterized as "ready, aim, aim, aim, ready, aim, aim, fire." We Methodists talked a lot, interpreted everything repeatedly but moved too slowly toward committing ourselves. Some members of a congregation will specialize as teachers, activists, or nurturers; but people who are responsible for larger oversight must embody all three leadership capacities. When we lead by keeping meanings, relationships, and structures well integrated, we create a greater possibility for generative, self-correcting praxis. In Aristotle's framework, if some set of activities is to be described as "praxis," then its ends are embedded in the current activities. This concept is behind the thought of Paulo Freire, who emphasized that action and reflection are interactive. By leading in this holistic and cohesive manner, we form and generate sustenance for the congregation in its vocation as a sign and agent of God's initiatives.

Once when I was leading congregational studies on Jesus's Sermon on the Mount, we were often troubled. Repeated attempts to understand these teachings about blessings, grace, and behaviors left us adrift and confused, yet lured. We studied the sermon in relationship to the whole of the Gospel of Matthew. We approached it in parallel with the Sermon on the Plain in Luke. Still, we were largely alien to the text. We read Bonhoeffer. We read Stanley Hauerwas and Will Willimon. Over several years, as our relational lives deepened and our involvement in mission increased, we kept coming back. Then one evening we began seeing the text in a very different way. That evening, the question was transformed from "What does this mean?" to "What kind of people do we need to be for this to make sense?" This is a different approach to hermeneutics, one that recognizes that not only do we interpret Scripture: it interprets us. That shift led to an overwhelming experience of convictions and longings about our lives—our marriages and families, our jobs and money, our politics and civic lives. God was forming us in the longer praxis of congregational life and mission. Note again the synergism, or creative interplay of relational, interpretive, and implemental leadership.

Are there deep congregational wounds or simmering volatility? Healing and redemption will require overlapping work on interpretation, relationships, and administration. Is it time for transformational change? Rerooting a congregation in classic narratives and practices, and forming new groups for study, caregiving, and mission will require the same multifaceted leadership. Does the congregation need to be lured away from complacency and complicity with consumer capitalism, careerism, and the role of chaplain to U.S. globalism? We have the grand hope of an alternative narrative, to be embodied in the relational and organizational practices of worshiping, learning, missional congregations. Leadership teams need to be formed and supported so that they thrive as participants and agents in God's redemptive reign.

Notes

1. Dulles cites sociologist Charles H. Cooley concerning these traits; see Charles Cooley, *Social Organizations* (New York: Schocken Books, 1909/1967).

2. See Josiah Royce, *The Problem of Christianity* (Chicago: University of Chicago Press, 1918/1968).

3. *Cohousing*, developed mainly in northern Europe, seeks to promote a more cooperative approach to housing that provides both private dwellings and common spaces and functions. For further information, log onto www.cohousing.org.

4. *Metanarratives* are large, overarching stories that provide meaning that smaller narratives do not have access to. While postmodernism looks askance at metanarratives and emphasizes smaller, local narratives, Christians can value those local stories while holding that the larger Genesis-to-Revelation narrative, and the Jesus story itself, are metanarratives in that they give meanings to the world beyond the texts' local specifics.

5. Emotional intelligence, or "EQ," is used in parallel with the more familiar intelligence quotient, or IQ. See Daniel Goleman, *Emotional Intelligence* (New York: Bantam, 1995).

What Kind of Pastor Will Most Likely Empower Laity?

EDWARD A. WHITE

It takes a certain kind of pastor to truly *empower* laity to discern and fulfill their God-given vocation in the world. What are some of the qualities of such a pastor?

1. A Pastor Who Is Secure in His/Her Sense of Self. One who is not threatened by those who seem bigger or smarter or stronger than they are.

Do you remember a book called *Anna and the King of Siam,* which was written by a Presbyterian missionary named Margaret Landon? It was made into a movie with Yul Brynner called *The King and I.*

In the movie there is a striking scene where Anna meets the king for the first time. She is taller than he is. He informs her that one of the rules is that no one's head must be higher than the king's. She dutifully stoops to oblige whereupon he stoops. She is required to bend even further until eventually both of them are kneeling with their heads on the floor.

How many times do our clergy leaders do this to their followers? Staff and laity get the message and are constantly stooping to oblige. How does this impact the people who are trying to grow in the faith . . . that is to grow up? Because they have not attended to their own inward journey, spiritually immature and insecure leaders stifle the spiritual growth of their followers.

Originally published in *Congregations,* vol. 20, no. 3 (May/June 1994), pp. 12–13.

By contrast I remember Bishop William Creighton. Some years ago he was the Episcopal Bishop of Washington, D.C. He stood six feet tall. But he was secure enough to relish attracting into the diocese many bright young clergy who were ten feet tall. He wasn't threatened in the least. He just supported them and rejoiced in their triumphs. The results included Tilden Edwards (who founded the Shalem Institute of Spiritual Formation), Loren Mead (who founded The Alban Institute), Jim Anderson (who founded the Cathedral College of the Laity), John Fletcher (who pioneered the InterMet Theological Experiment), and many more. One sign of spiritual maturity is when you are secure enough to help others become bigger than you are.

2. A Pastor Who Can Clearly Define Her/Himself. Can I state clearly where I stand and why without being judgmental? Can I speak with inward authority and send clear "I" messages?

The days when there was an automatic authority accorded to the clergy are long gone. People don't bow and bend anymore just because we wear our collar backwards. If there is any authority it consists of the personal authenticity and credibility that is grounded in the quality of our relationship to the community within which we serve.

I once heard an Episcopal priest named Jack Harris say, "Every pastor has to make a choice as to whether they want to be in control or whether they want to be taken seriously." If I want you to take me seriously I must surrender my control and give you the freedom and the permission to weigh my statements on their merits and to disagree with my ideas if they aren't convincing. Clergy need to care more about internal authority and less about external control.

3. How Grounded Is This Pastor in the Midst of Ambiguity and Conflict? Do I convey anxiety or the inner peace that passes understanding? How strong are my avoidance instincts? Am I able to live into and learn from the pain? Have I come to terms with my fear of death?

Rabbi Edwin Friedman says that clergy leaders have two primary tasks. One is to define where they stand on any issue in a clear, nonjudgmental way. The other is to remain connected to the members of the community in a nonanxious way as the people struggle with the issue, often in heated and anxiety-producing confrontations. The capacity to fulfill these two responsibilities rests on one's level of spiritual maturity.

The capacity of the community to deal with conflictive issues varies inversely with the anxiety level of the community. If the leader conveys anxiety it will escalate the anxiety of the congregation. If the leader conveys inner peace it can help to reduce the anxiety level of the community and thereby increase their capacity to cope with the issues.

4. How Clear Is This Pastor about His Own Possibilities and Limitations? Is the outcome of the struggle entirely up to me? (functional atheism) Do I, in the words of that great prayer, have "the courage to change what can be changed, the serenity to accept what cannot be changed and the wisdom to know the one from the other"?

I have a letter from God over my desk, It reads as follows: "Do not feel totally personally irrevocably responsible for everything. That's my job. Love, God."

What kind of inflated self-importance leads us to believe that human destiny rests on our shoulders? It is precisely that kind of illusion that compels many clergy to need to be center stage constantly in the life of their congregation.

5. Must Someone Else Lose in Order for This Pastor to Win? Can we share a victory together? Can I carry the banner of collaboration in a society that is compulsively competitive? Can I practice *solidarity?*

There is the World War II story of when the Nazis took over Denmark. They required all Jews to wear the yellow arm band with the Star of David so that they might be readily identified.

Then the King of Denmark, who was a Lutheran, put on a yellow arm band. When the king did it, all the Danes did it. Everyone was wearing a yellow arm band and the Nazis just couldn't tell who was Jewish. That's solidarity—the opposite of a society where the gap between rich and poor grows ever wider.

I'm told that many people experienced solidarity during the Great Depression. Testimonies went like this: "We were dirt poor then. But it wasn't altogether hopeless because everyone around us was dirt poor.

We all knew that we were in this thing together and that we had to see our way through it together."

That's solidarity. But somehow, after World War II when prosperity came to some in a big way and others stayed poor, the mentality of solidarity was replaced by the mentality of charity. "What must we do for them?" And as the rich have gotten richer, the answer has increasingly been, "Not very much!"

People need solidarity with, not charity from their pastor!

6. How Free Is This Pastor from the Constraints of Careerism and Consumerism? Am I clear about the difference between the *Gospel of Grace* and the *Gospel of Success* or the *Gospel of Self-Fulfillment?* What is the real ground of my sense of worth? What drives me? Does my compulsive workaholism convey a message of justification by works that drowns out my preached message of justification by grace?

The era of the "promised land" is over for the mainline church in America. Because we have not been faithful, we find ourselves again in the wilderness, or perhaps in exile. In either case the establishment is collapsing and with it the predictability, security, and comfort that has allowed us to be at ease in Zion for several generations. The model of the "king" is no longer appropriate for leadership in today's church. We need leadership more akin to the "judges" of ancient Israel who arose out of the community in crisis to lead by the consent of and in concert with the community. And those judges were selected not because of their caste or class, but their demonstrating the authenticity and therefore the authority that comes from having attended to the inward journey with God.

Pastors and Managers: An Executive Coach Assesses Leadership Skills

SCOTT EBLIN

Last year, after 15 years in management and a lifetime in the church, I left my job as a human resources vice president in a Fortune 500 company to answer a call that had been forming for several years. Through prayer and self-assessment, I realized that my gifts and passions centered around helping leaders identify their most important goals and create action plans for reaching them. I am now an executive coach working with leaders and managers in companies such as Capital One, NiSource, and Pfizer. But there is a twist to my coaching practice: I spend about 30 percent of my work time in churches with pastors and lay leaders.

As a coach drawing on both business and faith experience, I am struck by how lessons learned in one arena can be applied to the other.

The Shared Risk of Burnout

I have a theory that most pastors did not go to seminary because they had a desire to lead complex organizations. They went for reasons of call and from a desire to serve God through ministry. It is hard, though, to think of a more complex leadership challenge than pastoring the average church congregation. In *Personality Type and Religious Leadership*, Roy Oswald and Otto Kroeger[1] point out some of

Originally published in *Congregations,* vol. 27, no. 5 (September/October 2001), pp. 22–24.

the myriad roles that pastors are expected to play: leader, communicator, teacher, comforter, public relations manager, administrator, conflict resolution specialist, counselor, fundraiser, social coordinator, strategic planner, and trainer. That is an overwhelming list of responsibilities. When you add roles not mentioned by Oswald and Kroeger—such as manager, team leader, and coach—the list is even more daunting.

Most corporate managers are allowed to specialize and focus a bit more than the average pastor. Their jobs, however, are demanding in their own way. I have found that the overriding emphasis of managers is on achieving results, in areas like completing a project, reducing costs, increasing market share, or meeting earnings projections. In today's financial markets, results are framed in terms of calendar quarters, annual budgets, or three-year plans. Too often, the effect of this short-term focus is a sense of burnout and lack of purpose. Many managers are looking for a larger meaning in what they are doing, and most do not find it in the next quarterly earnings report.

Pastors, on the other hand, are working in the exact space where the burned-out manager should look for deeper meaning. As opposed to the manager's emphasis on results, the focus of most pastors is on relationships—at the most sublime level, on the quality of the congregants' relationship with God. Skilled and experienced pastors also seek to establish and strengthen relationships among their congregants. In relationship with God and others, the pastor's flock has the opportunity to find purpose and meaning in life.

But what of the pastors? The Alban Institute estimates that a large percentage of pastors suffer from emotional and career burnout. Many more experience some level of frustration in their work. Undoubtedly, there are many reasons for this. A common source of frustration for pastors is the feeling that they are not making the difference through their ministry that they had hoped they would. Put another way, they are not satisfied with the results they are seeing.

Relationships and Results

Many executives could benefit from stronger relationships, while many pastors could benefit from stronger results. Relationships and results both come from God. If we are in alignment with God's will, we can expect both strong relationships and positive results. As in most things, though, success is achieved through experience. In the areas of relationships and results, pastors and executives can learn from each others' experience. First, let me address what pastors can teach executives about relationships.

Ironically, the specialized knowledge and results-orientation that help most managers and executives rise to their positions are not enough to sustain them. Long-term success in the business world is based on fully applying one's talents to the accomplishment of meaningful goals. To do that, managers must show a sincere commitment to building relationships in the workplace. The best pastors model this relational orientation. They demonstrate it by viewing people as ends in themselves rather than means to an end, by listening for the hidden needs and hopes of others, and by helping people understand that they are loved and they are here for a special purpose that utilizes their God-given gifts and potential.

The ultimate role model in this regard is Jesus as a leader of his disciples. Think for a moment about how Jesus led the Twelve. He provided an inspiring purpose: "I will make you fishers of men." He took time to teach them through instruction and example. He modeled the behavior he expected of them. He gave constructive feedback and built them up. He was clear about what was most important. In the larger community, he included those who tried to do better and corrected those who limited the potential of others. In this way, Jesus built strong, empowering relationships with his disciples.

Learning from Managers

Pastors can learn from some common practices of successful, results-oriented managers. First, managers are very clear about goals and objectives: They understand what they are trying to accomplish and how they will measure the results. Second, they communicate these goals and standards, so that everyone is clear about expectations and accountability. Third, good managers understand that their role is to set direction and coordinate the work of others rather than to do all of the work themselves. Fourth, when problems or issues develop, effective managers address them sooner rather than later. Finally the best managers provide feedback to their team members. When things are done well, they point that out, applauding actions that support the goal and encouraging the team to stay the course. Conversely when a team member's actions do not support the goal, effective managers explain why a change in approach is required.

The steps that successful managers take to get results are not necessarily at odds with the relationship-building skills shown by the best pastors. To the contrary, I believe that a well-grounded approach to achieving results combined with a sincere relational orientation is the foundation of both healthy businesses and healthy congregations.

Goal Setting

Goals provide focus as well as guidance in resource allocation. In setting goals together, a congregation defines its priorities. Like leaders in business, pastors must guide their congregations in setting priorities. As part of the goal-setting process, the pastor should ask questions of the staff, lay leadership, and other congregants that will help everyone prayerfully determine what success looks like.

Clarifying questions might include:

- What opportunities has God put before us?
- How do our gifts and resources equip us to address those opportunities?
- What do we need to accomplish to fully meet those opportunities?

By involving a representative cross-section of the staff and congregation in goal setting, pastors can build commitment and accountability around the church's priorities. Likewise, it is vitally important for pastors to actively involve the congregants as the church's priorities are addressed.

The list of pastoral roles presented earlier in this article match up fairly closely with the various spiritual gifts Paul discussed in his letters. It is important to remember that while all of us have gifts, none of us has all the gifts. This is as true for pastors as it is for laypeople. By involving the laity in accomplishing congregational priorities, pastors free themselves to play from their strengths while enabling others to grow in their own gifts.

Constructive Feedback

As people work together to accomplish a goal, they need to hear regularly what is going well. Pastors can play an invaluable role in spiritual and leadership formation by unhesitatingly and publicly offering sincere praise as congregants and staff achieve results and build relationships.

On the other hand, very few undertakings go smoothly from start to finish. Making adjustments and corrections is part of the process. Because of their relational emphasis, pastors are sometimes reluctant to call for or take corrective action as soon as it is needed. But, when offered in the spirit of Christian love, correction can be a valuable component of spiritual growth. Again, Paul provides strong examples of this in his letters to the church at Corinth. In his first letter to the Corinthians, Paul takes the believers to task for their infighting and lack of focus on what is most important. As chapter 12 concludes, he writes, "And now I will show you the most excellent way." From there, of course, he writes a beautiful description of the behaviors that together compose Christian love. In these chapters, Paul provides a model for giving good feedback in a tone that is firm yet loving.

In following Paul's example, pastors should offer constructive feedback in private and in a timely fashion. A reliable method is to point out to the recipient the behavior that is impeding progress, note its impact, then assure the person of your support going forward.

Lessons to Be Learned

When intent is pure and purpose is clear, pastors can sustain and even strengthen relationships while seeking results. In the end, sustainable results, whether in the business world or the world of faith, are facilitated by rich communication. Goal setting, role clarification, accountability checking, and constructive feedback are all functions of good communication. When practiced with love and compassion, this kind of communication always builds up relationships.

Pastors can learn from business executives to intentionally apply communication tools to achieve results in Kingdom work. Executives can learn from pastors how to be more relational as they strive for results. When leaders in any field bring together a relational orientation with a results orientation, good things begin to happen.

Note

1. Herndon, Va.: The Alban Institute. 1988.

Telling the Better Story

GIL RENDLE

Research has shown that leaders of large congregations deal with much more complex daily management issues than do small church pastors. But how do they do so while still providing leadership that shapes a community of faith out of a diverse group of gathered people? This question is still being explored, but one answer that appears to be emerging is that effective visionary leaders of large congregations tell stories.

In a stunning article written in 1987, J. Gordon Kingsley, then president of William Jewell College in Liberty, Missouri, tried to answer the question of what a college president does.[1] Naturally, he acknowledged all of the business of leading: the meetings, the phone calls, the handshakes, the presentations, the dinners, the budgets, the spreadsheets, the personnel issues—the list goes on. But, having summarized the activities and tasks of a president, Kingsley made the claim that all of this is still not at the heart of what a college president *does*. In claiming the central purpose of the president's role, Kingsley turned to images of the bard, the poet, "the solitary singer galvanizing a people to noble, even heroic action by the power of Their Story."[2] With conviction, and with a suitably convincing telling, Kingsley wrote that the real work of the president is to learn the story of the college in order to tell its story—to help others find their place in that story, so that they can become participants in writing the college's next chapter. Kingsley was

---

Originally published in *Congregations*, vol. 31, no. 1 (Winter 2005), pp. 23–26.

pointing to the critical difference between all of the management activities that determine *how* an organization fulfills its purpose and the
critical leadership skill of being able to give voice to *why* an organization fulfills its purpose.

I would argue that Kingsley's thinking has direct application not
only to colleges and their presidents, but also to congregations and
their leaders. Learning, telling, and rewriting the story of the congregation is, I believe, a key and critical practice of leadership in the large
congregation that needs to be understood more deeply.

Attention to congregational size confirms that leaders in large congregations must develop more administrative and organizational forms
of leadership. This shift challenges the management skills and capacities of many large congregation leaders, who are suddenly responsible
for a complex organization with often competing differences and a
sensitivity to quality and performance—all of which can no longer be
negotiated by simply getting people together to agree, as is often done
in small churches. Indeed, it is essential for large congregation leaders
to master many of the organizational and administrative tasks named
by Kingsley as the responsibility of a president of a college. But still we
are not talking of leadership—of what makes the community "hum,"
gives action purpose, gives faith meaning, makes ministry live.

Increasingly, I believe I am watching leadership surface in a new
way as leaders tell the stories of their congregations. The effective use
of story is leadership that goes well beyond efficient and effective organizational management. To be sure, large congregations require effective management, but a well-run organization does not call a person to
personal searching, nor a community to reach beyond its own comfort
for greater purpose.

The Power of Story

In the story of Esther in the Hebrew Bible, Mordecai learns
of a plot to destroy the Jews. Haman, an officer of King Ahasuerus,
plots against the Jews because Mordecai, himself a Jew, will not bow
down before him as did all the other servants of the king. When
Mordecai, knowing that all will be lost if the king is not alerted, charges

Esther with going to the king in her role as queen to plead on behalf of the Jews, Esther shrinks from the task because she has not been summoned to speak with the king, a considerable problem since those who speak uninvited are subject to death. But Mordecai is not put off. He retells Esther's own story in a way to empower and embolden her. "Who knows?" he says. "Perhaps you have come to royal dignity for just such a time as this." In his retelling he shifts Esther's understanding of herself from one of powerlessness as one of the servants of the king to a position of power in which she sees herself in a role of royal dignity. She is moved from fear to courage—all in the retelling of who she is.

Powerful stories do not need to be long and elaborate. Jesus, walking by the Sea of Galilee, came upon two brothers, Simon and Andrew, who were fishermen. "Follow me," he said to them, "and I will make you fishers of men." In this very brief retelling of Simon and Andrew's stories, Jesus used simple wordplay (from fishermen to fishers of men) and the first disciples answered the call and set out to do things they had never before dreamed of.

There are modern-day examples of the power of even the simplest story, as well. For instance, in a community divided by factions, one congregation realized that they were a safe place for all parties to meet, so they began to tell their story as the town "meeting place." This retelling of their place in the community shifted them from a passive role to one of active ministry in reconciling groups with contentious differences.

Howard Gardner, professor of education at Harvard University, writes that when one thinks of the leader "as a storyteller, whose stories must wrestle with those that are already operative in the minds of the audience, one obtains a powerful way of conceptualizing the work of leading."[3] Gardner says the visionary leader doesn't just rehearse or retell an existing story but, having learned the story of the people, actually creates a new story that produces change. Jesus took simple Galilean fishermen and gave them a better story to live: as fishers of men. Similarly, the "better story" told effectively and embodied authentically by the leader of the large congregation galvanizes, directs, and provides leadership.

Old Centers No Longer Hold

The people participating in large congregations are less and less able to find a common center around the links that once held people in congregational community together. Personal family relationships, ethnic identity, a shared denominational history or identity, polity—the way of "doing church"—or a neighborhood location were ways in the past by which the people in a congregation could share a commonly held center. While these centers can still hold in smaller congregations, they have, for the most part, disappeared in the large congregation. People are drawn to large congregations for the multiple opportunities and choices among programs, for the alternative worship settings they represent, and for the small group connection with others like them that they offer, all of which underscore the differences that people bring to the congregation rather than providing a common center that all share.

Increasingly, what seems to form the new center in the large congregation is the story—the narrative of who we are as a congregation, as a people of faith. The story that one large congregation tells is of being a place where people of great theological and social differences can gather, but where discernment and decisions will come from their center as a part of the reformed Christian movement. People of great differences in this congregation know that they are welcome, but that their congregation will behave in a way guided by tradition. The story that another large congregation tells is one that begins in the moments of high risk taken during the turmoil of the national civil rights movement in the United States. Participants know that their congregation, true to its history, will continue to seek social justice on a wide number of fronts, not all of which they will agree upon. To be sure, there are many smaller stories in each of these large congregations that serve as examples and evidence of how the larger story of "who we are" rings true. The power of the story in the large congregation is that people can share a sense of "belonging" as long as they can see themselves in and as part of the larger story, yet they do not need to be in agreement or share great similarities with everyone else.

In one large urban congregation in the middle of a large metropolitan city, where people of very great differences live day by day, the central unifying story is one of the gathering together of great diversity. Members of the congregation see their church as having received this location as a gift from God, so they include in their congregation a very wide range of people of different ages, races, economic means, genders, sexual orientations, nationalities, political alignments, and theological backgrounds, and they encourage people to hold these differences proudly. Like many large congregations, they are able to hold all the tension of their differences because the individual participants do not need to engage all of these differences directly. Participants can appreciate the differences present in the congregation, but because the congregation is large and provides multiple small groups and task forces with focused purpose, individuals can make their deeper connections in subgroups of people that they find to be much more like themselves.

The idea of a fully diverse congregation and the visible witness to their differences can easily be seen in public moments, such as times of worship. But members and participants in the large congregation do not need to reconcile all of these differences. Diversity can be appreciated in the large gathering and in the identity of the congregation. But individual participants then commonly participate in small group programs with the people with whom they have the most in common— such as the people focused on public policy, the people centered on spiritual healing, the people who are gay and lesbian, or the people committed to neighborhood mission. Reflecting on the tension between the diversity of the whole and the similarities sought out in smaller groups, the senior pastor observed that "belonging" is never negotiated in the congregation. As long as individuals are able to see themselves in the congregation's story about the inclusion of the great differences in God's creation they can both participate themselves and welcome the participation of others who do not share their particular interests or life experiences.

Connection, Resonance, Meaning

Clearly, leadership is not telling people what they want to hear. It is not creating the story with enough "spin" to manipulate people for personal or congregational advantage. Leadership happens when the leader tells a story sufficiently healthy, authentic, and purposeful for others to feel connection, respond with resonance, and find greater meaning. Connection happens when people are able to say to themselves, "I see myself in that story." Connection seems not to rely upon full agreement or a need for compliance from others. To feel like a part of the larger whole seems to be enough.

Resonance suggests that the historicity or accuracy of the story is not as important as the question of whether or not it rings true. When the story rings true it enables the listeners to generate a new way of thinking and acting that embraces—and even advances—the truth the story represents.[4]

Meaning suggests that a purposefulness is found in the story. We increasingly understand faith and religion as a doorway to creating meaning in our lives. Much has been written about the spiritual search for meaning that has taken hold in a postmodern, post-9/11 world that found materialism and consumption to be empty and science and technology to be incomplete by themselves. The life-giving story has to point beyond ourselves and our congregation to some greater purpose. As such, the empowering story of the congregation must be connected to the much larger story of our faith.

Telling a Congregation's Story

How do leaders provide story leadership? The most probable answer to that question is that they do so intuitively. Good leaders in large congregations seem to just know the power of story and intuitively learn to use the congregation's story to shape the community and guide ministry. Narrative theory applied to organizations, institutions, and community has not been public long enough to give a rich language to this leadership by story. Nonetheless, there is a structure and a process that leaders bring to the authentic telling of the story. In this brief article, that structure might be captured simply in the notion of learning, challenging, and collaborating.

The first movement of leading by story is to learn the story that is currently being lived. This is leadership by listening—listening to how a people talk about themselves: the metaphors they use, the way in which behavior and attitude do or do not match their words, the memories captured and retold, and also the memories forgotten or denied. The leader, at this stage, does the homework of the objective, or dispassion-ate, learner, whose task is to capture the larger picture of this congrega-tion in the real context of its own history, its changing environment, and in a shifting culture. The leader learns what is said and unsaid, seen and unseen, and willingly searches for connections to the biblical text and to spiritual practices.

Having listened, the leader then begins to tell the story of what was learned. In this second movement of leadership, the retelling task of the leader is always directed to helping the people find and live the "better" story of their future. To be in relationship with God, who be-lieves that we can ever be more than we presently are, means to submit our stories of who we are to the challenge of the story of who we might be. So the leader shifts from the listening mode to the talking mode. As the story is retold, the leader challenges whether there can be more or less to the story—more health, more depth, more meaning, or less fear, less caution, less control. This period of challenge produces anxiety for all, including the leader. When our stories are challenged our identity is questioned, and this is experienced as a moment of chaos. What was once known is now uncertain, and what was once home is now wilder-ness. We all do not behave at our best in such anxiety, so the leader must provide support and safety along with the challenge of the retell-ing in order to help the people stay with and live into their new story.

The third movement of leadership by story comes as leader and people together use what they have learned to collaborate on the new telling of the story or the writing of its next chapter. Some large con-gregations use formal planning processes at this collaborative stage. Planning is a prime opportunity for the congregation to rehearse the formation questions of ministry that rest at the center: Who are we? What has God called us to do? Who is our neighbor?[5] Some leaders use focusing moments such as leadership retreats since these are times to step away from daily duties and consider the "big picture" that al-lows for thinking about the future in a new way. Leaders will com-monly use the established paths of structured conversations that come out of sermons, teaching moments, staff meetings, and governing board discussions. The new telling or the next chapter often has the energy that ignites passion in people, and a clarity that attracts people. In the large congregation, the new story does not always have all members' agreement. In fact, the new collaboration is often the product of and dependent upon the ongoing argument and accommodation that will continue into the future as a way to shape and sharpen the story.

But Is It Leadership?

The North American assumption of leadership is that it must be decisive and directive, a kind of leadership in which the single leader points a direction that others cannot see. Leaders in large congregations do need to be decisive and able to make decisions at appropriate moments. But the truer act of leadership in the faith community—particularly in large, diverse congregations—is to stand with a people to discern together a future that is faithful to God's call. The importance of shaping and claiming the story of identity and purpose in the large congregation stands out as even greater than the management tasks of budget, personnel, and program development. It is the leadership that stands at the center of the congregation.

Notes

1. J. Gordon Kingsley, "The President as Bard," *AGB Reports*, July/August 1987, 18–21.
2. Ibid., 18
3. Howard Gardner, *Leading Minds: An Anatomy of Leadership* (New York: Basic Books, 1995), xi.
4. Stephen Denning, *The Springboard: How Storytelling Ignites Action in Knowledge-Era Organizations* (Boston: Butterworth Heinemann, 2001), 38.
5. Gil Rendle and Alice Mann, *Holy Conversations: Strategic Planning as a Spiritual Practice for Congregations* (Herndon, VA: Alban Institute, 2003).

Dimensions of Pastoral Authority: What It Means to Become a Congregation's Pastor

CHRISTINA BRAUDAWAY-BAUMAN

After intense years of study and sacrifice, he turned in his last seminary papers. The master of divinity diploma is framed, ready for hanging. Behind him also are the yearly meetings with the denominational committee whose interrogations earnestly and prayerfully sought to discern his fitness for ordained ministry. After all the affirmative votes were counted, a worship service was held in which he made promises so large they could only truthfully be answered, "I will, with the help of God." Hands heavy with hope were laid upon his head and a stole was placed around his shoulders. Now called to serve his first congregation, his mail begins to arrive with the title "Rev." on the address label. The word "pastor" is printed beside his name on the church's signboard outside on the street corner and in the Sunday morning bulletin. He climbs the worn steps to the pulpit on his first Sunday and breathes a sigh of relief, believing he has, finally, fully arrived. In his first small attempt to begin to make a mark on this congregation's life, he had replaced the ink sketch of the church's building on the front cover of the worship bulletin with a graphic that illustrated his sermon topic. Immediately following the service, as he shakes hands with the members of his new church, more than one asks with concern what other changes he plans to make. Deflated and baffled, the new pastor wonders what, if anything, he has done wrong, and what this might mean for his future in ministry with this congregation.

This illustration is not an isolated incident. My experience in the past three years working with nearly 80 new clergy—both as the

Originally published in *Congregations*, vol. 32, no. 4 (Fall 2006), pp. 42–46.

coordinator of a pastoral residency program at the Wellesley Congregational Church, United Church of Christ, and as the associate for new clergy development for the Massachusetts Conference, UCC—has revealed that nearly all new pastors have some more or less dramatic version of this story to tell from their first encounters with their congregations. Only recently, however, as first-call pastors have come together in small groups designed for their reflection and support, have they begun to recognize this experience as common and to see in it an opportunity to gain a clearer understanding of what it means to become a congregation's pastor. The conversation often settles on exploring the meaning of "pastoral authority." We have come to see that pastoral authority is not just one thing. It has several dimensions, which I have come to name as granted, earned, claimed, borrowed, and shared.

Pastoral Authority as Granted

There are some denominations, and certainly there are congregations, in which the authority of the pastor is more naturally assumed—where, for example, the congregation grants a pastor permission to make changes or decisions on his or her own. The truth, which remains largely unspoken, however, in seminary classrooms, in the process toward ordination, and by local church search committees (even by those who claim they are looking for strong pastoral leadership), is that in most places very little authority is simply granted to pastors new to a congregation.

There may be many reasons why a congregation would feel hesitant to immediately grant such authority. Much has been written already about how the status of the church has shifted in our current culture. The church, after all, does not hold the same honored place in civic life that it did even a generation ago. It follows that the pastor does not either. Though the church building may still sit on the center of the town green, the church and its pastor now rarely reside at the center of influence in a community's life.

I am convinced that gender, age, and a congregation's history also play a role. Although the number of ordained women has increased exponentially in recent years, it is still true, though thankfully not everywhere, that congregations are often slower to grant female pastors authority. Young pastors are also often granted less authority than second-career clergy, though their number of years in ministry may be similar. Congregations who have had a healthy relationship with a previous pastor may be willing to grant authority more easily. Churches that have suffered a breach of trust in relation to a former pastor will naturally grant a new pastor less authority.

One of the most important factors in how much authority a congregation grants is theological. One of the central tenets of the faith and polity in churches of the Reformed tradition is the "priesthood of all believers." Our fundamental commitment to this Protestant doctrine makes us wary of an understanding of ordination that marks a distinction in status or substance, elevating someone above others. Each congregation is a priesthood of believers, which has a life that is more than a mere collection of individuals. It has a history of defining moments, traditions it holds as sacred, aspirations it yearns to achieve, practices that reach to the core of its identity, and a faith that may be expressed in its own peculiar way. "The priesthood of all believers" does not mean that the congregation will not recognize the calling and priesthood of the pastor, but the role of the pastor needs to be defined in relation to the particularity of the congregation he or she has been called to serve. Congregational consultant and author Roy Oswald has repeatedly advised any pastor new to a congregation to begin by becoming a historian of a congregation's life and to take time to discover its norms and values before jumping in to making changes.[1] In response to the concern raised when he changed the bulletin cover on his first Sunday, John Hamilton, the new pastor of First Congregational Church, UCC in Norwood, Massachusetts, did two things. He immersed himself in reading the archives of his new church, and reflected back to the congregation in sermons and meetings what he was learning. He also established the practice of inviting church members one by one to have coffee with him at a local café. Following a predecessor who had served this church for more than 30 years, John understood how important it was for him to get to know as fully as possible the congregation who had called him.

By contrast, however, many new clergy are so eager to use and prove their gifts that it is often only after they have made missteps in leadership—and perhaps even alienated their first congregation—that they realize their actions could be perceived as less than respectful. When a new pastor revamped the church school after hearing dissatisfaction with the former curriculum but without discovering what parents and children had appreciated about the old way of doing things, she later recognized that it was difficult for members who had poured their energies into the former program not to feel criticized by the dramatic change. This was true even though it was a successful shift by any other account. When another new pastor began his ministry by rearranging the parts of the worship service into an order his seminary had taught was more theologically sound (without first engaging the congregation in conversation), committed members of the church no longer felt that worship was in their voice. For them, it was no longer "liturgy," the work of the people, and some long-time members began to leave.

Pastoral Authority as Earned

Another word for pastoral authority is trust. Very little of a congregation's trust is simply granted. Mostly it is earned. As a pastor consistently—day to day, Sunday to Sunday—leads worship faithfully, offers care compassionately, affirms the gifts of others, equips members for ministry, and assists the congregation in making wise and faithful decisions, she earns their confidence. Pastoral authority that is granted focuses on the pastoral office; pastoral authority that is earned has more to do with one's character, with the congregation's observations of the pastor's behavior, and with relationships—not only the pastor's relationships with individuals but also his or her relationship with the congregation as a whole.

It takes time to build trust, lots of time. Even after many years of serving the same church, this trust, which is essential for a congregation and pastor to accomplish anything together, can rarely be merely assumed. The work of building rapport and nurturing relationships, of considering who else needs to be involved in the conversation and in making decisions goes on continuously. Attentive pastors quickly learn that patience is an important pastoral virtue.

So is love. When a congregation knows that their pastor loves and respects them, trust grows. After serving for a year as a pastoral resident at the Wellesley Congregational Church, Nicole Lamarche remarked that one of the things she knows now that she didn't know when she started ministry is that "first and foremost my job is to love the congregation that has been given to my care. All of the other pieces of ministry are almost meaningless without this. Certainly my call to be prophetic will fall on deaf ears without the love."

The pervasiveness of conflict in church life comes as a surprise to many new clergy. Over time, wise pastors come to see conflict not only as inevitable but also as a potentially creative dynamic. Members of the congregation watch how a pastor interacts with viewpoints different from her own and how she copes with emotionally charged situations. Whether she reacts defensively in anger or calmly and thoughtfully can mean the difference between resolving a conflict and causing it to escalate. When arguments erupt, it is incumbent on the pastor to be one of the people in the room exhibiting the least anxiety. Staying centered and connected even when tempers flare contributes enormously to helping gather the trust of a congregation.

Emotional maturity is an essential pastoral quality, not only for engaging in conflict but also in every interaction a pastor has with his congregation. Every pastor loses some battles. Losing them with grace sets a tone for the whole congregation. Loving every member of the congregation, even those who are the hardest to love, is an important part of pastoral identity. It is also a powerful Christian witness.

Pastoral Authority as Claimed

Recognizing the difference between a decision that a pastor has the authority to make and one that the congregation needs to consider is a skill that comes with experience, sometimes after many trials and errors. Often it depends on the style and practice of a particular congregation. There are times, however, when a pastor needs to step in and claim the authority of the office to which she has been called.

When a premarital couple becomes mired in the details of creating a show as a bride and groom, it is the pastor's role to step in and recover the wedding as a worship service, an expression of covenant commitment and God's own faithfulness to us. When a bereaved family becomes overwhelmed by trying to incorporate into a service all the people who have something to say about their lost loved one, it is the pastor's

role to claim the funeral as first and foremost an assurance of the promises of God. When a congregation is lost in conflict, with members focused on trying to convert one another to their own points of view, it is
the pastor's role to guide the church into a process in which members
can instead discern God's point of view together.

Sometimes claiming such authority calls for courage. For months,
one congregation wrestled mightily over whether or not to become open
and affirming of gay and lesbian people. Members who normally got
along relatively well were locked in heated debate and became very upset
with one another. Insults were exchanged and people lost their ability
to listen to one another. In all this time, the church's pastor never told
the congregation where his own faith called him to stand. He was concerned that if he did so it would sway the congregation one way or
another, and some would criticize him. The problem is that they were
already divided and there was no one who was providing direction.
Although the pastor was earnestly trying to be respectful by serving as
a disinterested peacemaker, I believe he neglected to claim the authority that was his call to claim and that his church needed him to claim.
The congregation flailed around in the dark, while the person holding
the flashlight—the person charged with the responsibility to help them
interpret the Gospel and to listen prayerfully for the leading of the Holy
Spirit—neglected to turn the flashlight on.

Congregations do rely on their pastors to set a loving tone, to discern the right questions, to offer a thoughtful perspective, and to shed
a glimmer of light in the midst of confusion. This does not mean that
the pastor always knows what to say or do. But every pastor needs to
claim from within him- or herself the authority that comes from a clear
sense of calling to ministry in and on behalf of the church. While it is a
call to lead, it is not a call to have all the answers. Sometimes stating
loud enough for everyone to hear that the way is not yet clear is a deeply
faithful answer. There are occasions when saying "we need to pray about
this" is even more so. And when a pastor thinks she might have the
answer, or is sure she does, this is the time when she needs to be especially attentive to which kind of authority she is speaking from and
how she is being heard. Is she merely offering her own opinion? Is she
amplifying voices in the congregation who may not otherwise be heard?
Is she allowing room for other perspectives that may be just as faithful

as her own? Most importantly, the pastor's role is continually to bring God into the room, to bring the resources of the Christian faith to bear on the congregation's life, and to help the congregation listen for God's guidance.

Pastoral Authority as Borrowed

The greatest source of pastoral authority, then, is not granted by a particular congregation or earned by personal integrity. It is borrowed from the Christian tradition, from the church, from the Gospel, and from Jesus himself. In fact, it is safe to say that all other forms of pastoral authority are derivations of this one.

John Thomas, the general minister and president of the United Church of Christ, puts it this way: Understanding that ordination "is the authority conferred by the church to represent the ministry of the whole people of God… reminds us that ministry in general and ordination in particular belong to the church and not to the individual." Pastoral authority is a "conferred authority that is, in a sense, 'on loan' to the individual."[2]

Perhaps the power of borrowed authority is exhibited most clearly when there is a death in the congregation or the community. At such a time people look to the pastor to be the one to offer some good news. It is not the preacher's eloquent words, however, that mean the most to them. It is the Word that comes from God, the Word that carries God's presence and comfort in grief, and God's promise of eternal life. By this borrowed or representative authority, pastors are invited to be the ones to bless others at funerals and bedsides, at baptisms and weddings, and to stand in the pulpit Sunday after Sunday serving as a point of intersection between our human longing for God and God's desires for our lives.

While carrying such authority is itself a blessing and an awesome responsibility, it can also sometimes feel like a burden. As one new pastor realized after one of her first encounters with a member of her congregation, "clergy can be a lightning rod for a lot of things." The day after she had invited her congregation in prayer to come before God "holding the New York Times in one hand and the Bible in the other, fully aware of all the troubles and burdens in the world," she received an irate e-mail message from an angry parishioner who took her *Times* reference to be an endorsement of the newspaper's editorial viewpoint. In reflecting on this experience with her peer support group of other new clergy, she came to see that "people project onto you all kinds of things simply because you are a pastor." All pastors receive many kinds of criticism and praise. Only some of either actually have anything to do with them.

Most pastors would do well to remember that their ordination is not their possession. It is an authority that the church has loaned to them as a trust to be held with reverence and great humility. Because pastors are permitted, by virtue of their role, very privileged access into people's lives, their intentions must be honorable, their speech and actions respectful. Pastors hold the safety and well-being of the church and its members and are called to make themselves into safe harbors, worthy of the confidence others place in them.

Pastoral Authority as Shared

The final form of pastoral authority brings us back to where we began, with the priesthood of all believers. No matter how remarkable or well-rounded the gifts of a particular pastor may be, ministry is always a communal project. It is the work of the people, not just the pastor. Offering care to the members of the congregation, for example, is not simply something the pastor is called to do. Rather, the role of the pastor is to care for the whole congregation in ways that enable all the members to recognize that caring for one another is their common calling. Similarly, it is not the pastor's work to set the agenda or to determine the vision for the congregation. Instead, it is the pastor's role to work with the congregation to create an environment in which members can together discern God's vision for them and take the risks to which God is calling them. Our apprehension of God's work in the world is made richer when there is room for the experiences of all the gathered to find expression. God's realm comes closer when the gifts of all the faithful are acknowledged and nurtured and used.

Ultimately, ministry is a gift that God shares with us. The church is given its calling and its tasks by God, who boldly places faith in us. Ministry is our response to God's extravagant grace. Excellent ministry, then, is less about anything we ourselves might accomplish on our own and more about what God is able to do through us as pastors and congregations together.

Notes

1. Roy Oswald, James Heath, and Ann Heath, *Beginning Ministry Together: The Alban Handbook for Clergy Transitions* (Herndon, VA: Alban Institute, 2003), p. 64.
2. John H. Thomas, "Something More: Authorized to Represent," presented at the Ministries Issues Convocation, March 7, 2002.

Power Principles for Pastors

ART GAFKE AND BRUCE MCSPADDEN

Imagine reading the following headline in your local Sunday newspaper: *Power Brokers Invade Local Churches.* Would you recoil in horror or cheer?

What role does and should power play in the church? Power is one of the least discussed issues in the church, but if you can read these words then you must be alive, and to be alive is to have power. Power refers to the basic energy to "be" and "do." Power itself is amoral; what we do with power determines its value.

Unfortunately many in the church believe in the ethic of the righteous loser. We are more comfortable talking about serving and being last than about being powerful. This understanding misleads us to believe that exercising power is sinful. But power is a Gospel gift. Jesus's charge to pick up one's cross and follow invites us to use our power. Seeking to save ourselves usually happens when we *avoid* asserting our power. Recall the words of Luke: "Then Jesus called the twelve together and gave them power and authority over all demons and to cure diseases, and he sent them out to proclaim the kingdom of God and to heal." (9:1)

Jesus was anything but weak. He powerfully proclaimed the Gospel mandate for the poor and it got him chased out of his hometown synagogue. Jesus cast out demons, overthrew the money changers in the temple, and even challenged the ultimate power of death and won.

Originally published in *Congregations,* vol. 20, no. 4 (July/August 1994), pp. 10–13.

Was Jesus just different or has God also offered this empowering legacy of power for the church and its ministers to utilize as an expression of God's presence in the world? The fundamental question we must answer is not "Do we have power?" The question we must answer is: "Will we claim the power God has given us?"

First, let's take an inventory of the power that may be laying dormant just beyond your fingertips.

Forms of Power

Access to money is power. Money talks. While most churches regularly bemoan a lack of money, financial power refers to more than having a large bank account. In the mathematics of power, the equation that says that money is power does not imply that the lack of money is the absence of power. Financial power is also having the resources to supply whatever people need or want. Drug dealers understand this principle: controlling something people crave gives even the most inexperienced kid on a street corner power over someone else. Unfortunately since money is often used to have "power over" people, churches shirk from powerfully using the finances available to them.

Churches often see themselves as poor and powerless. But what other institution has the opportunity to use its financial resources as "power for" meeting the needs of people? What is often needed is a new look at the *real* financial power of the church. For instance, when the churches of one denomination in a major American city assessed their church properties they discovered a combined worth of over $50 million. Church leaders began to see that they had financial responsibility and leverage of which they never dreamed. By banding together they had the kind of assets that would allow them to confidently work with bankers and business persons on cooperative urban efforts.

Many pastors and congregations see fundraising campaigns as a necessary evil. Yet the need for money should be understood as an opportunity and stimulant for the church to vitally address the needs of its congregation and community. Fund raising gives the church a chance to invite the congregation to talk and act upon community needs and valued commitments.

There is power in numbers. When people band together they have the power of a collective voice. Rarely do we take full advantage of this powerful resource. A rural pastor unknowingly stumbled upon this power when he wrote in the weekly newsletter that a local convenience store owner had pressured the town council to not allow a new youth organization to relocate next to the store. The pastor simply asked the church people to consider whether or not it was an act of good stewardship to spend their money in a store that did not value constructive programs for the town's teenagers. When the owner of the store heard of the pastor's simple sentence she quickly retracted her opposition to the youth center. The owner feared the pastor's power to influence a significant number of people and how they spent their money. The pastor was dumbfounded, but he learned that the power found in numbers can be used to influence the world for good.

Information is also power. The scandal over insider trading on Wall Street revealed the power of information. It isn't just "who" we know that builds power, but "what" we know as well.

Pastors have access to information that makes them very powerful. Often pastors know what parishioners give to the church and consequently have a good idea of family income. Additionally, parishioners entrust pastors with confidential and very personal information. Just as the stock brokers misused their knowledge for personal gain, some ministers do as well. This fear of exploitation often causes other pastors to shy away from bold ministry that intentionally increases power for the good of the community.

This shirking is hardly in keeping with the Gospel gift of power. Abdicating power is as harmful to building the church as is misusing power.

Skill is a means of power. When we know how to do something that needs to be done, we have power. In organizational work it is the task of the pastor to continually seek to build the power of the church. To speak of building the church's power is often suspect. If a pastor seeks to "build" a congregation of 2,000 members, ministerial peers and current congregational members are often suspicious and wonder, "Is this pastor on a power trip?" Again, this liability leads too many pastors to forfeit the power that is available for fear of being misunderstood. Building the power of the church isn't primarily about attracting large Sunday morning crowds; a truly powerful church is one that teaches and enables each person involved to use and refine his or her skills, thereby unlocking the influence each one can have for good in the church and community.

One local pastor determined to build her church's power through a visitation program. She set up a discipline of dividing her visitation time three ways. One-third of her time was spent with parishioners, one-third was allocated to getting to know city, county, and community leaders, and the final third was expended in making cold calls to the homes around the church. Her intent in visiting the neighborhood was to discover why people chose to live in the area, what they liked best, and what they felt were the most pressing problems of the area. This discipline both honed the pastor's interpersonal and community organizing skills *and* built the power of the church. By taking the time to listen to the community she collected information about the needs of the community and emboldened trust in her as a leader in the area. That pastor understood that true leadership is the willingness and ability to use her skills in building up the church.

There is power in holding institutional office. Pastors often fail to recognize the power that comes from claiming the title of "Reverend." Think about it. People voluntarily attend worship and willingly listen to a sermon preached by the pastor. People ask the pastor to pray for their needs and then become silent and listen attentively. People offer their money to pay for the pastor's salary. Holding ministerial office opens the doors to hospitals, prisons, and schools. Congregants come to the pastor with their pains and seek help. People call on the pastor to be present in times of greatest joy and deepest sorrow, thereby sharing their vulnerabilities.

Additionally there is the sacred power to administer the sacraments to the faithful. Who else is given the power and privilege of representing Christ on the people's behalf?

The next time you hear a pastor claim to be powerless challenge that assumption. Many remain in denial about the great power the office itself holds. Rather than being powerless perhaps that pastor is abdicating the call to claim the Gospel gift of power.

In the United Methodist ordination service, the bishop says to each new ordinand, "Take thou authority." The bishop doesn't bestow power but offers it to be claimed. If any minister fails to take this power he or she won't have it, not by design but by failure to responsibly use power to further God's purposes in the world.

The Disciplined Use of Power

Clearly the church has access to many forms of power. For power to be used wisely requires discipline. The undergirding truth that all of us must recognize is that human power can only be understood in the context of God's power. God is the creator of life and the power source. It is our task and calling to accept the gift of power within the context of a disciplined Christian life.

Spiritual disciplines and power. The spiritual disciplines of meditation, prayer, and worship help us focus on God as the source of our life and power. As we remain in close connection with the divine source we guard against being controlled by our narrow self-interests and we open ourselves up courageously to take the risks that are associated with the exercise of power.

Relational discipline and power. The relational disciplines of love keep us vitally connected to others. The disciplines of accountability and interdependence allow our lives to be mirrored back to us by others. When we share our plans, hopes, and failures with others our motives and strategies for action can be refined so that any use of power can rightly be used for the good of the many. Beware of any pastor or Christian that makes unilateral decisions and refuses to be yoked in decision making with other faithful believers. "Lone rangers" can easily become power happy and lose sight of the goal of empowering others.

Institutional discipline and power. Institutions by nature have checks and balances built into them. Committees are responsible to boards and staff members are given policy manuals to guide their actions.

Admittedly some religious institutions sometimes seem more like over-
loaded trucks spinning their wheels mired in mud than like efficient
vehicles, but rather than discounting the institutional framework, any
powerful leader must creatively learn to use the structure for the benefit of the church. After all the structure is comprised of people. Building trust and extending relationships outward is one of the main tasks
of any pastor. A powerful leader will come to understand that the people
working within the institution can become powerful allies for making
change and doing good.

So if we all have access to more power than before imagined, and
we can courageously use this power within the context of a spiritual
life, how then is power best used in the church?

The Proper Use of Power

Power within the church is more like manna than dynamite.
Just as the early Israelites had to go out early in the morning and harvest just enough for that day without storing or hoarding the manna,
power is best used regularly and not stored up for one great show of
power. Each day power is provided; there is no need to save it for difficult days when we aren't getting our way.

Here are three principles for regularly exercising power that serve
to strengthen the church.

Power doesn't come from the top down; it comes from the bottom up.
Claiming power has nothing to do with getting uppity; real power comes
from getting basic—which means getting back to the roots. A powerful
pastor and church share the characteristic of constantly evaluating actions according to the basic reason a church exists. The church as an
institution is meant to serve people. Whenever the church loses its focus you can bet that the power being wielded is being used for less holy
purposes.

Most of us can think of ready examples of churches which have
lost the vision. Here's one more to add to the list.

A district Superintendent went to meet with the congregation of a
church ready to split over the use of the church facility by a day care
center. When asked to whom the mission of the church was directed

neither faction could answer. Instead they were intent on cannibalizing themselves, eating their small congregation alive, in order to be right over this one issue.

Soon a new pastor was appointed with the mandate to refocus the church on ministry. He skillfully challenged the church to assess the needs of the surrounding community and to direct its funds toward meeting those needs. As the congregation became mission focused, the day care dispute worked itself out. The congregation, when focused on serving people, forgot about being right and became intent on making a difference.

The goal of powerful leadership is to enhance all those involved. Dividing churches or "burning out" pastors by putting them in losing situations is not a wise use of either personal or institutional power.

Power grows when shared. Building personal power or the power of the church is not enhanced by working longer and longer hours. The way to do more is for more people to be called into relationship with one another—not by the pastor being spread too thin. A powerful pastor must focus his or her time on the activities that organize people to achieve common goals. Rather than trying to "get the job done," a task that is impossible for pastors, the focus becomes "What can I do that will extend relationships, empower people, and build the church?" Any task or opportunity, when seen through these priorities, then becomes a building block in the construction of a powerful church that serves the broader community. No longer does a pastor have to feel fragmented by the urgent matters that too often seem like disparate activities. Rather, with this focus the pastor can feel whole even in the midst of the diverse demands.

A seminary intern showed how effective the principle of sharing power can be. While working in conjunction with a small senior citizens group, the decision was made to offer a forum on health care for seniors. The intern could have spent a significant number of hours on the phone to pull together a group of medical experts to come in and talk to the seniors. Instead she gathered together a group of eight of the senior citizens and organized them into a design team for the forum. Those eight people took responsibility to recruit speakers and participants, and as a result nearly sixty people attended the forum. Their success also motivated the design team to stay together to organize future projects. Instead of putting on an event, a base community was formed that continues today, long after the seminary intern returned to her studies. Individual church events can become a pastoral burden and an end in themselves or they can become opportunities to extend relationships, empower people, and build the church.

Stay within the range of your power. The final principle of using power warns against using power foolishly. Exercising power is a risky business that demands great vulnerability and self-honesty. A pastor who decides on the afternoon before the annual church meeting to change the major emphasis of church ministry without allowing for the church leaders to process the changes is working outside the range of his or her power. Going into a significant meeting without getting the wisdom and support of others is a misuse of pastoral power. If the pastor's desired changes go down to a resounding negative vote or gain a grudging victory, his or her ability to lead will be diminished. In all probability both pastor and congregation will go home frustrated and depressed.

One's range of power is determined by the resources, skills, information, and web of relationships one has developed. Power and the ability to lead increase as power is shared. When the power base is strong, there will be little need for a pastor singlehandedly to radically change the direction of a church—the necessary changes will be understood and sponsored by many.

A Portrait of a Powerful Leader

The biblical story of David and Bathsheba aptly illustrates the difference between ably using power and misusing power. David, as king, had successfully used his power by accompanying his troops into battle. Then one spring David decided not to fulfill his duties as a military leader by fighting alongside his soldiers. David chose to stay in Jerusalem. Soon thereafter, one afternoon while walking about on the roof, David saw Bathsheba bathing nearby and he wanted her. We all know the rest of the story. David, knowing full well that Bathsheba was married to a soldier engaged in battle, took her. Perhaps he thought, "Isn't it my prerogative to have what I want? After all I am the king of

Israel? Who will ever know?" By exercising his power for personal gain rather than Israel's, David placed himself at great risk.

But misuses of power have consequences, and David soon was entrapped in a scheme of deceit to cover up his first abuse of power. Uriah, when called home, remained faithful to his military commitment and refused to visit Bathsheba. Uriah exercised his power against the wishes of the king to remain faithful to his duty to country and comrades. So David wielded power and arranged for Uriah to die. In these acts of abusing power, thought to be personal and private, David took his family and Israel on downward courses. Any misuse of power has personal, relational, and institutional consequences—both in ancient times and today.

In this same story, however, Nathan comes on the scene and provides a clear example of a courageous and wise use of power. In following God's directive to confront David, Nathan puts himself at great risk. His very life was at stake; David could have had him executed. But Nathan stayed within the range of his power. He did not walk into the royal chambers and directly accuse David as an adulterer and murderer, instead he appealed to the just sensibilities of David as king by telling a parable of a poor man unjustly robbed of that which he loved. David himself became involved in the story and became his own accuser.

Nathan wisely used his power as a prophet and problem solver as an opportunity to bring David to personal repentance and restoration as a wiser, chastened king.

Nathan showed great audacity and great faith. He put himself at risk in order to further God's purposes. In theological terms. Nathan's power was greatest when he chose not to shirk using his power out of a desire to protect himself from the possibility of death or failure. Instead Nathan claimed his power, used it wisely, and radically reordered sacred history. How can we do less? The same power is available to us today. Who among us is willing to claim power and use it to God's glory?

The Myth of Competence

ISRAEL GALINDO

Excellence does not require perfection. —Henry James

The Rev. Susan Finster stood at the back of the church greeting her parishioners at the end of her first "real" sermon at her first "real" parish. After seven years as an associate pastor at two congregations, she had started the day excited about her first Sunday as the new senior pastor of Miles Road Church. The service went well, and from all accounts the sermon was well received. Susan took to heart the compliments from the members.

"Great sermon, Pastor," said a member of the search committee.

"Well done," a deacon added.

"Thank you," a young mother said. "That's just what we needed to hear."

But not 20 minutes later Susan found herself in her office, weeping. She was replaying the sermon in her head, focusing on points in her delivery she thought were poorly done. She wondered if anyone had noticed that her pulpit robe was too large. She fought back a familiar queasy feeling in her stomach that was always accompanied by a small critical voice that asked, "Who do you think you are, anyway?" Fighting the conflicting emotions that boiled up, Susan ended the morning angry at her inability to celebrate the day and her accomplishments. She wondered again at this constant feeling of inadequacy.

Originally published in *Congregations*, vol. 29, no. 1 (Winter 2003), pp. 17–19.

Clergy have one of the most challenging careers anyone could hope for. And despite theologies of grace and callings to servanthood, congregations expect performance from clergy. This expectation to perform and to get "results" can become a point of personal and congregational anxiety. Poorly managed, such discomfort can result, ultimately, in clergy burnout, termination, and congregational frustration. It does not help that American congregations live within, and often share, a culture whose values reflect corporate "bottom-line" attitudes and expectations of leadership. As a result, clergy themselves often take on these performance expectations.

I have identified, among leaders in both secular and religious contexts, what I've come to call "the myth of competence."

The myth of competence is the attitude, fed by chronic anxiety, that engenders the belief that personal self-worth, relevance, and meaning reside in *external* definitions and assurances of being competent in all that one does. It manifests itself in ways of functioning and relating in the church that can result in burnout and depression.

What the Myth Is Not

I do not imply certain understandings, nor should they be inferred, when I speak of "the myth of competence." First, I don't mean that incompetence should be tolerated in congregational ministry. In fact, for clergy in a senior leadership position, tolerating incompetence merely ensures that it won't be long before the congregation loses its best people. Neither do I mean that we should not be good at what we do. We should, in fact, be setting an example of doing our best for the Lord and the church, employing our gifts and talents.

The myth of competence does not mean that we should refrain from challenging people to higher standards, or fail to hold them accountable to clearly communicated performance expectations. We should not make excuses for laziness. Truth be told, lazy people can have a great capacity to use good theory to poor ends. I can't tell you how often I've heard people use the concept of self-differentiation to say, in effect, "That's not my job," or "I don't want to overfunction."

The Roots of the Myth

The myth of competence is a particular occupational hazard that haunts people in leadership, in both corporate and ministry contexts. The myth stems from issues related to a sense of self-worth, a personal formative history, a deficient belief system, and a lack of fully realized self-differentiation, or self-actualization. The myth also involves the context and relationships in which leaders find themselves.

If Susan is to overcome her tendency to embrace and function out of the myth of competence, she will need to realize that the myth operates at both personal and systemic levels. While it resides at the individual level, it is also a systemic issue: it manifests itself fully in how a person functions and relates to others at corporate levels. The myth shows itself in relationships at work, in the family, and in social and community environments.

Susan has long suspected that her nagging feelings of inadequacy began when she was a child. She's not far off the mark. Erik Erikson's theory of psychosocial development demonstrates that issues of competence are central during a formative stage of life. Erikson called the fourth stage of development "industry vs. inferiority." This stage occurs during our elementary school years. At this developmental stage we become keenly aware for the first time, overtly, of family emotional processes, including parental expectations, the performance demands of school, and messages from peers. Participation in competitive sports serves to confirm that we are not all created equal in skills and abilities.

Because of the nature of congregational relationship systems, people who function from a belief in the myth of competence are susceptible to unhealthy relational and communication patterns. Those pathologies take advantage especially of leaders who fail to act from a strongly self-differentiated stance. These leaders are ripe prospects for chronic anxiety in various manifestations—"hostage-taking" ("If you don't perform better, we will judge you"), a myopic focus on issues and content ("It's the pastor's preaching that's the problem"), "identified patient" strategies ("It's the *pastor* who's the problem"), and feelings of dependence ("I'd better not rock the boat; no one else will accept me if I fail here").

Symptoms of the Myth

People who buy into the myth of competence suffer predictable symptoms. For Susan, the ones that often got her into trouble as an associate were oversensitivity to criticism and inappropriate responses to flattery. The former gave "power" to the critics in the system and derailed her ability to provide vision. The latter tended to make her emotionally dependent and susceptible to seduction.

Other symptoms include a hypercritical attitude toward others' successes or failures, and a tendency toward blaming (which puts the focus on "others" and fosters "deflecting" repertoires like excuse-making and passive-aggressive behaviors.) Negative feelings about competition are symptoms, as are feelings of persecution, inadequacy, insecurity, and "shame."

The myth of competence makes some clergy reluctant to take risks. This hesitance leads to a failure in leadership and can, in turn, contribute to a lack of personal and institutional growth. Ultimately such clergy are unable to provide vision, often engaging instead in "poll-taking" leadership and never-ending consensus building. Others ultimately tend toward reclusiveness and timidity, as well as overfunctioning or underfunctioning.

The Paradox of the Myth

Clergy and congregations can fall victim to societal values that focus on success (typically meaning more and bigger) and "results." Miles Road Church, Susan's new congregation, has a reputation for demanding top-rate performance from its clergy and staff. It is also known to hold high expectations for the standard of worship (especially the preaching), the excellence of the day school, the use and appearance of the buildings, and the quality of programs.

Maintaining high standards is a desirable corporate value, but when it is motivated by anxiety it can the trap clergy or congregations in the myth of competence. In that case, the drive to maintain standards becomes the drive for perfection (or the appearance of perfection). Such attitudes embody a certain paradox. Rather than resulting in confidence in the leader, they result in insecurity (you can't always "act" your way into a new reality, which is what Susan found herself doing). Rather than resulting in effective leadership, insistence on near-perfection results in weak leadership because it feeds into "sick" systemic forces driven by anxiety. Rather than liberating the leader, it oppresses—having to be "perfect" all the time is exhausting! Rather than enabling mission, the standard of perfection fosters myopia because leaders focus on their performance as judged by other people's expectations.

The paradox of the myth of competence is that rather than generating freedom, it leads toward controlling behavior, since a leader focused on competence has little tolerance for honest criticism. When the focus of leadership is on the appearance of competence, it results not in personal and congregational growth but in stagnation. Once we find the comfort zone of a repertoire or "bag of tricks," we will tend to stick with it and not risk opening ourselves to the challenges of growth.

While those who live by the myth of competence can maintain the façade for a while, the end product is the opposite of what is desired. Rather than resulting in maturity, this mode of leadership leads to dependence. Leaders whose primary aim is to appear competent always have their radar turned on, scanning for other people's approval. Rather than resulting in differentiation, this approach results in enmeshment as we become overdependent on the system to provide affirmation of our self-worth, our values, and our vision. Ultimately, rather than focusing on functioning better, we become preoccupied with appearances. Leaders whose drive comes from the myth of competence are more concerned with appearing competent than with leading effectively. They'd rather receive the affirmation of congregants than engage in challenging the congregation's system toward maturity, growth, and integrity.

Moving toward Wholeness

How do we move beyond swallowing whole the myth of competence? For individuals, overcoming the myth may be a lifelong struggle, especially for people like Susan. On a corporate level, systemic anxiety, dysfunctional relationships, and power issues complicate the picture. Perhaps the most productive starting point for moving toward wholeness begins with the leader. Here are some suggestions:

First, confess incompetence. Given what we are called to do in ministry, we are all inadequate to the task.

Adopt a functional theology of grace. Living with the myth of competence may express the lack of ability to receive grace, leading often to an inability to extend grace.

Make personal excellence and relevance the standard of your ministry, not competence. There is a qualitative difference between a driving desire to appear competent and a commitment to excellence. Excellence involves setting standards based on your own values and principles rather than working to meet other people's expectations. The chart on the next page contrasts these two postures.

Accept failure as progress toward a goal. You know you're doing better if you are willing to accept the risk of failure as a step in the process of achieving goals and visions. Leadership requires vision, vision calls for risk, and failure is often the price paid en route to realizing one's vision. Learn to risk the cost.

Seek to understand the source of the myth of competence in your life. One's family of origin is a good place to look. Where and from whom did you get the message that you were not good enough? That you would "never amount to anything"? Children whose parents live vicariously through them are prime candidates for the myth of competence.

Redefine the role of leadership. Leadership is not being perfect, or infallible, or "strong," or authoritative, or "the best" or "most important." Leadership is about providing the appropriate functions needed by the church at the right time, promoting health, maturity, and differentiation in others. It means challenging the system more than it means keeping people happy.

Given what we are called to do—preach like a golden-tongued angel every Sunday; run an organization efficiently using a volunteer force and depending on donors' generosity; afflict the com-

Competence-focused Leadership	Excellence-based Leadership
Locus: External	Locus: Internal
Characterized by anxiety	Characterized by enthusiasm
Feeds on deficits and insecurity	Feeds on challenge
Informed by external standards	Informed by internal values
Responsible to others	Responsible to self
Driven by external expectations	Driven by internal impetus
Global and vague	Selective and specific

fortable; give care to souls that may be unwilling and unmotivated; lift a countercultural prophetic voice in an often hostile (or worse, apathetic) culture; and act as God's presence at all times and in all places—given all these demands, we will always be inadequate. No one is competent by oneself to do all that is required for successful ministry. The good news for the Rev. Susan Finster, and for us, is that we are not called to do it alone, and that our primary calling is not to results, but to faithfulness.

Committing to Mutuality:
An Interview with Eugene Peterson

DAVID J. WOOD

Eugene Peterson is perhaps best known for his 20 books, including *Under the Unpredictable Plant: An Exploration in Vocational Holiness* and his paraphrase of the Bible, *The Message*. His primary vocation has been the pastorate. He "planted" a new congregation, Christ the King Presbyterian Church in Bel Air, Maryland, which grew to 500 members in his 29-year tenure.

I traveled to the home of Eugene and his wife, Jan, in Lakeside, Montana, for a few days of conversation about his understanding and experience of pastoral life. I settled quickly into the Petersons' comfortable home on the shores of Flathead Lake, and into the Sabbath-like pace. For 30 years, the Petersons (now parents of three grown children) traveled here every summer from Maryland to return to their Montana roots and to be refreshed by the beauty and serenity of the land. After retiring from Christ the King and teaching spiritual theology for five years at Regent College, Vancouver, British Columbia, Eugene came home. Here he would complete his translation of the Old Testament.

Recently Eugene, with Jan's full support, took himself off the speaker's circuit. It was time to give up pulpit and podium for pen and paper. He is as certain now as he was throughout his pastoral ministry that if he is not rooted in time and place, his words and witness will lose their gravity He dwells in a place of solitude but not of isolation. He and Jan provide hospitality to a stream of family and friends. They are active in a local Lutheran congregation. Eugene spends time with

Originally published in *Congregations,* vol. 28, no. 3 (May/June 2002), pp. 4–7.

pastors, helping them reflect on their work. The couple's life is uncluttered by e-mail or TV.

Peterson, raised a Pentecostal in Kalispell, Montana, was the son of a Pentecostal pastor mother and a butcher father. (He played high school basketball with Pentecostal classmate Phil Jackson, who later won fame as a coach in the NBA.) After college, Eugene set off for New York, where he attended Biblical Theological Seminary (now New York Theological Seminary). Though his sojourn from Pentecostal to Presbyterian began in fall 1954, Eugene's Pentecostal roots would continue to nourish his theological imagination.

While earning a master of divinity degree in English Bible at BTS, Eugene coached a winning church basketball team at Madison Avenue Presbyterian Church, where the celebrated George Buttrick held forth.

Eugene earned a second master's degree at Johns Hopkins University, Baltimore, in Semitic languages. Married and with a family on the way he took a pastorate in White Plains, New York. Yale University, within commuting distance, accepted him into its Ph.D. program in Old Testament under scholar Brevard Childs. But before beginning his studies, he realized where his vocation lay: "I am a pastor." His turning to the pastoral life was not a renunciation of intellectual life or of his passion for biblical languages. But from then on his service to the church and his intellectual flourishing would be shaped by the pastoral vocation. In 1962 the Baltimore Presbytery asked him to start a congregation, and his long ministry began in earnest.

David Wood: Eugene, what's your reading of the current "clergy self-care" movement?

Eugene Peterson: My initial response is that it narrows the context of pastoral work and identity. I'm wary of the term "self-care." We're such incorrigible, selfish persons that I'm loathe to give it a fancy term that makes it OK.

Maybe the most important thing I did as a pastor in this area was not to assume that I needed to protect myself from the congregation and its supposedly insatiable demands. Instead, I sought to foster a collaborative relationship.

How did you do that?

Here's what I said: "Help me. I have needs. I can't function well without help from you. We're in this together, we're doing the same thing, we're worshiping together, we're living the Christian life together. You've asked me to do certain things to help you do it—to lead you in worship on Sunday, to visit you when you're sick, to help administer the church. But I need help in all of this." I worked to create conditions in which this kind of collaboration would flourish. For example, I would take my elders and deacons on retreat twice a year, and we'd spend 36 to 48 hours talking. We'd talk about needs—their needs and mine, and how we could help each other do what needed to be done. They became very imaginative and sensitive, coming up with things I would never have thought of.

It sounds as though you would not separate "self-care' from "congregational care"?

Right. From time to time—three or four times a year—I would write a congregational letter on topics such as "Why your pastor keeps a Sabbath," "Why your pastor reads books," "Why your pastor stays home with his family on Friday nights." I wrote about these practices not to seek approval or to justify what I was doing with my time, but to invite [members] into the same kinds of practices—practices that should matter to all Christians. This kind of writing helped me remember why these practices were so important to my life as a pastor, our life as a family, and our life as a congregation.

Once I wrote a letter titled "Why your pastor never repaired his television set." Again, I didn't do it with an attitude of moral superiority toward television. I simply related our experience as a family and how positively our life together was shaped by the choice not to repair our TV. Of course, there was an implicit invitation in the narrative: "Next time your TV breaks, try leaving it broken for six months and see what happens."

In what ways is the pastoral life unique?

One thing unique about this life is that no other calling has quite as much intimacy in it. This is where things can go wrong for pastors. Intimacy is vulnerability—it's a place where there could be much betrayal, exploitation.

One way to deal with this danger is to refuse the intimacy and say, "I'm a functional pastor. I'm not a relational pastor." You may succeed as a manager or a program director, but you will fail as a pastor.

If you're going to negotiate this tricky terrain of intimacy, you must have a strong commitment to mutuality. It's not exactly like a marriage, but there are parallels. It is precisely the demand of intimacy that many pastors find so hard to sustain.

What allows you to stay in that intimate engagement and not be overcome by it?

A term that occurs in the literature of the spiritual masters is "detachment." Now detachment is the cultivation of a relationship that is present, but not taking ownership, not being messianic or managerial. It gives the other person freedom—it allows the "other" to be "other."

This way of relating requires detachment from a "need-based" relationship. It is inherent in the gospel, but it's easy for it to get skewed by sin or co-opted by sin in the guise of compassion. I love the phrase in T. S. Eliot's *Four Quartets*: "Teach us to care and not to care."

Caring, but not caring. They're both part of the same thing. It's an art. You make mistakes along the way. You don't learn it in your first year in the parish.

It sounds as though you are not going to hold a congregation responsible for what is your responsibility. At the same time, you won't let them hold you responsible for what is their responsibility. Coming to this kind of understanding must take some effort.

It has to be learned, and it has to be learned without assuming an adversarial position. I refused to let any of this become adversarial. I'm even a little hesitant to use the word "negotiation" to describe the process I have in view. We're friends. We're brothers and sisters in Christ.

If you can see your relationship with parishioners as friendship "with mutuality and affection," that undermines the hierarchical structure almost from the beginning. People feel that they're being valued for their own sake, not for what you can get out of them or how you can use them.

That is why I insist on the importance of a pastor's going to people's homes—because you're on their turf. They're the host. You're the guest. It's hard to maintain that hierarchical function when you're at their mercy.

That's one way a pastor can practice mutuality rather than talk about it.

Yes. Friendship is at the heart of it. There's a lot of talk about spiritual direction these days, which is good. But spiritual direction at its best is friendship—that is, paying attention to somebody with affection and appreciation.

Over 15 or 20 years, I was in the homes of parishioners three or four times. These visits were not prompted by crises—they were simply pastoral visits. When I left my congregation, I realized that many of these people had come to think of me as their best friend.

That didn't happen because we did things like playing golf together or going to ball games. Friendship grew out of the way we learned to pay attention to one another's lives over time. In many ways, it was this kind of relational work that kept me from burnout.

I don't think pastors "burn out" because they work too hard. People who work hard often do so because they're good at what they're doing and they enjoy doing it. I think burnout comes from working with no relational gratification. Relationships become laborious and draining. Pastors can lose touch with relational vitality when their relationships are driven by programmatic necessity. When this happens, pastors can lose the context for love, hope, faith, touch, and a kind of mutual vulnerability. In the midst of the congregation, pastors become lonely and feel isolated—and that isolation can be deadly to the pastoral life. Those are the conditions in which inappropriate intimacies flourish.

I think the epidemic (if it is an epidemic) of sexual misconduct by clergy has less to do with clergy overindulging intimacy or not being careful about intimate relationships, and more to do with the absence of genuine intimacy

Many pastors I know who are vital and alive to their work have an unmistakable relational quality. It strikes me that there is little space in their lives for inappropriate relationships because they are so oriented by good relationships.

That's right. I think "self-care" requires caring well for others. One principal way to keep your sanity, your health, and your emotional equilibrium is to care for somebody else.

I can remember times when I felt hemmed in or felt that I couldn't do this work anymore. One way I got through those times was to care, in very deliberate ways, for someone else. It's amazing how caring for someone else helps you forget about yourself.

Let me shift gears here. Sabbaticals are widely regarded as a principal strategy for sustaining good ministry over the long haul. As I recall, you had one sabbatical in 30 years. In your 24th year of ministry, you spent 12 months in Montana with your wife, resting, reading, and writing. But ordinarily you had two months a year

away from the congregation—in Montana. Part of that time was vacation and part was study and writing. That strikes me as an annual sabbatical rhythm. How did this rhythm shape your practice of ministry?

My congregation always gave me a month's holiday. And then, on their own, the session [church governing board] decided to give me an additional month for writing. They didn't ask me. They didn't consult me. They just gave it to me. It was part of that "help me" sort of thing, except I hadn't said "Help me" right then. I'd write for a month, and I'd just be with the family.

The 12-month sabbatical I received was, again, a "help-me" thing. I told them I would like to stay there [in the congregation] forever if they wanted me, but I didn't think I could do it without a sabbatical. They were generous and gave me a 12-month sabbatical. When I came back from time away, I was energized, fresh, and ready to go.

How would you contrast or compare the rhythm of standard sabbatical policies to the two-month annual arrangement you had?

I was grateful for the annual rhythm. In the Presbyterian Church, we're given a month's vacation and two weeks' study leave. People work hard on those study leaves. You're supposed to produce something. It wouldn't be that much different to add two weeks to it and tell pastors, "Do anything you want to do. Read. Go to a monastery. Photograph wildflowers. Write." For me it would be to write, but not everybody's a writer.

The almost total incomprehension by our society of what a pastor does puts pastoral identity at risk almost every day. Two months would not be inappropriate vacation and leave for the needs we have.

Those annual two months away must have been sustaining.

Very much so. One of the side benefits from my annual time away was that it developed a competent lay leadership. Over the years I did less and less of what ordinarily is seen as what pastors do. The laypeople did it very naturally, easily, because they were trusted. I think it's important to trust people to do things. They're not going to do it the way you did it. They are going to make mistakes, but you make mistakes too.

There is no question that any strategy of clergy "self-care" must include the development of a competent congregational leadership.

Let's talk for a minute about the engagements you had beyond the congregation. Throughout your ministry you taught in a seminary/university context.

Teaching was a natural for me. It was what I loved to do, and I was in a place where there were schools. I just happened to be in the right place at the right time for somebody to know who I was and what I was doing.

I'd teach one semester a year, either spring or fall. I taught at a university, a seminary, usually alternately. I have often wondered, if I had been in a rural place with no schools for 500 miles, or even 50 miles, what would I have done? Was there anything I could do other than that? I think I would find a place to work part time that wasn't too demanding that would put me in a different environment for a few months a year, or a half-day a week.

I have a friend who lived in farming country Every summer he worked in the fields at harvest time. He worked half a day for six weeks. But he got to know farmers. It was totally refreshing for him.

Your teaching placed you in a different setting and role. I don't hear you suggesting that these engagements should be thought of as a way to escape the parish.

Oh, no. It was to feed the parish, actually. I never felt that teaching drained energy from pastoral work. If I had felt that, I wouldn't have done it. My main work was the congregation. This was a way to bring fresh blood into it.

Another engagement beyond your congregation was your weekly gathering with a group of pastors for lectionary study and collegial conversation.

That was an important part of my pastoral life. It became part of the rhythm of our life. The pastors who did this with me still call me and write to me about how significant and sustaining it was for them.

When did you meet?

Every Tuesday they'd come to my study at noon. They would bring a bag lunch. I'd have a coffeepot. We met for two hours. We were serious about what we were doing but not terribly disciplined. There was small talk. Sometimes somebody would come with a personal crisis. We'd drop everything and just spend the time listening and praying.

The group included a variety of pastors and backgrounds. There would be 15 or 16 in the group, and fewer than half were Presbyterian. We had Presbyterians, Pentecostals, and Roman Catholic priests. We even had a rabbi for a number of years. It was very ecumenical. What brought us together was a conviction that preaching was the primary task we had to do, and we wanted to do it as well as we could.

Most of the time when we met, we would focus on the lectionary texts for the coming Sunday It varied from the Old Testament to the Epistle to the Gospel, every season. We wouldn't necessarily preach on the texts we discussed. It was the discipline of being together around the Bible, thinking preaching, thinking sermon, thinking interpretation, that was highly significant.

I can imagine that the group came to think of one another as friends.

We'd often have one evening a month, Friday evening usually, when we'd have a potluck supper together. Another significant thing we did: in late spring, as close to Pentecost as we could make it—we never met through the summer months—we would take a day away together for a silent retreat. We would end the day with the celebration of the Eucharist. Even though we did that only once a year, it did a lot to build the solidarity of the group. It was a culmination of a whole year of relationships, prayers, and conversations.

A Congregation of Mystics: Reigniting Our Passion for Encountering and Experiencing God

N. GRAHAM STANDISH

I've always felt something has been lacking from our modern churches, something essential. Growing up I acutely felt this lack, which drove me to leave the church at 15. People like me thirsted for spiritual water, an oasis in the midst of life's desert. Our thirst was expressed in our questions, questions that the church didn't seem to hear, let alone address: "Where is God in the midst of suffering? How can we experience God personally? How do I hear God?" Like so many other spiritual nomads of my generation, I wandered and sought God elsewhere. I returned only when I found that the new age philosophies and spiritual movements of the day offered only mirages.

In the early 1980s I went to seminary, hoping to find spiritual water, but everything I studied seemed so dry and lifeless. It wasn't until after seminary that I finally discovered the spiritual water I had been seeking. I discovered it in the upper balcony of a little bookstore in Pittsburgh, Pennsylvania, where I found the writings of Christian mystics from throughout the ages, writings I explored more deeply a few years later during my doctoral studies in spiritual formation.

The writings of these mystics helped me digest the dry, creedal, and systematic theology of the mainline church. Reading the writings of mystics like Dorotheos of Gaza, Francis of Assisi, Catherine of Genoa, Julian of Norwich, Meister Eckhart, Teresa of Avila, John of the Cross, George Fox, John Wesley, Horace Bushnell, Hannah Whitall Smith,

---

Originally published in *Congregations,* vol. 31, no. 2 (Spring 2005), pp. 23–27.

Thomas Kelly, Catherine Marshall, C. S. Lewis, and Henri Nouwen offered answers to so many of my questions, for they rooted their theology and answers in an experience of, rather than speculation about,
God. They saw church as the place of a living encounter with God rather
than a place ruled by an ethical, moral, theological equation: *Live according to the Bible and the Golden Rule, study the Bible, say that Jesus
Christ is your Lord and Savior, and win a free trip to heaven.* What the
mystics spoke of was an encounter and experience of the Trinity that
transforms life.

The Christian Mystical Tradition

What is a mystic? Theologians have tried to define mystics
for centuries. Unfortunately, most mistakenly define mystics according
to their ascetic lifestyles, prayer practices, or mystical experiences and
visions. These are not what define mystics. They are a byproduct of
what mystics seek in their lives, which is to live according to Luke 10:27
by seeking to love God with everything they have and to love others as
themselves. Their pursuit of a loving relationship with God defines them.
They devote their lives to the quest for God and God's love, and this
quest leads them to uniquely live, pray, and experience God. It is a mistake to think of a mystic only as a person living a cloistered, contempla-
tive life, for many mystics live busy, active lives, but in a way that is
centered in God. Whether we are talking about the teachings of the
Desert Fathers and Mothers, the confessions of Augustine, the medi-
eval musings of Bernard of Clairvaux or Meister Eckhart, the theological explorations of Martin Luther, or the stories of C. S. Lewis, mystics
have continually pointed out that God can be encountered, experienced,
and united with through love, prayer, and the cultivation of the fruits
of the Spirit (Gal. 5:22–23).

How do the experiences and writings of the mystics intersect the
life of the church? Mystics reside at the center of every major Christian
movement. Point to any true renewal movement within any denomination, a movement that actually leads people to encounter and experience the triune God, and you will discover mystics at their core,
proclaiming their message that God can be tangibly and passionately
sensed, discerned, and embraced throughout life. Mystics have always

led people to follow their example of surrender to, uniting with, and serving the Trinity. Unfortunately, the church hasn't always listened. In fact many of these mystics were criticized and sometimes even persecuted (like John of the Cross, Meister Eckhart, Martin Luther, and George Fox) for preaching this message of a personal experience of God.

Church Resistance to Mystical Tradition

Too many of our modern churches have lost a passion for God. They have become functional rather than spiritual. They function like organizations whose main task is offering religious programming rather than as a body incarnating and opening people to God's presence. Ministry in these churches is dominated by functional concerns over organization, programming, and adhering to tradition for tradition's sake. They forget that ministry has to have a spiritual aim to be truly transforming and lead people to Christ.

The people of today yearn for much more than just a functional, routine set of rituals and practices. They want to encounter the Trinity in deeply spiritual ways, but their churches and denominations seem blind to their yearning. A 2003 survey conducted by the Presbyterian Church (USA) Research Services reveals this blindness.[1] The survey found that spiritual formation was an integral part to a "very great extent" (42 percent) of church members' lives, which suggests a deep spiritual hunger among our laity. Yet only 6 percent reported that spiritual formation was to a very great extent an integral part of their congregational life. Less than 2 percent reported that it was to a very great extent an integral part of the life of the larger judicatory bodies or the denomination as a whole. This survey certainly has its flaws, and represents only one mainline denomination. Still, the findings suggest that there is a serious disconnect between the spiritual lives of individuals and the openness of congregations and denominations as a whole to a more spiritual approach.

Why do so many mainline churches persist in emphasizing functionality and the routine when members are hungry for spiritual nourishment? Part of the answer lies in the leadership of our congregations. When leaders, both pastoral and lay, are called forth at every level of the denomination, they generally are called based on their functional abilities: Does he have experience in management? Is she organized? Does he have the technical skills for this committee's work? Does she have the ability to get things done? We rarely ask where these leaders are spiritually. We rarely ask whether they pray and believe in prayer, how much they believe that God can be encountered and experienced, or the extent to which they have faith that God will bless the church and cause great things to happen. In effect, we don't generally call mystics to lead mystics.

The Quaker spiritual theologian Thomas Kelly says that at the core of every church lies a "blessed community,"[2] a community made up of mystics centered in prayer, who sense God's presence throughout the church, and whose faith sustains those around them, even though they may be largely unnoticed by the larger congregation. They are generally not the people we call to lead the church, yet they are the ones sought out by the members when they are struggling, in pain, and need to sense God's presence in their lives.

So many churches resist calling these people to lead precisely because these mystics emphasize the experience of and service to God over everyday functioning. Their primary orientation is living in the kingdom of God in the here and now, while the primary orientation of many of our functional leaders is the "real" world—the world of business, political, and organizational life in which God seems to have little role to play. It is difficult to ask people whose everyday milieu is a world without God to lead a church into the kingdom of God. This does not mean that only mystics should be called into leadership, for not every mystic has leadership qualities, but spiritual openness should be a primary quality we look for in leadership. The best alternative, of course, is always to call leaders who have their feet firmly planted in both camps, people who are mystics operating in the "real" world.

Fanning the Mystical Embers of a Church

So how do we lead a church to become a community of mystics living in the kingdom and the real world? There are specific practices and techniques churches can adopt, such as offering spiritual retreats, classes on prayer, and programs on the spiritual disciplines.

Adding these to a church's program may promote greater spiritual awareness, but they can also become more of the same—functional programs that now have a spiritual bent. Congregational transformation requires more. It requires a new way, a more spiritual way, of doing church. The following are specific ideas that can help transform the church, some of which are expounded upon in greater depth in my book *Becoming a Blessed Church.*[3]

Mystical Leadership

To expand on what was said in the previous section, the transformation of our congregations requires that we call forth leaders, both pastoral and lay, who are open to the mystical and the spiritual. This means that the pastors of a church must have a passion for encountering and experiencing God the Creator, Son, and Holy Spirit in everything. When the pastors of a church have this passion, it allows them to lead a church to move in a more spiritual direction.

Still, the pastor cannot do it all. A pastor can set a course, but lay leaders must move the congregation toward its destination. What the pastor can do is lead the church to seek lay leaders who share a passion for God and prayer, are willing to listen for God's guidance, are aware of Christ's continual presence all around them, and can walk in faith, trusting in the power of the Holy Spirit to bless their work and the congregation. Pastors can also train lay leaders to connect their faith with their leadership. While there are resources available to help with this, many of which are available through the Alban Institute, much of this work is also new to the life of congregations, and requires that pastors and leaders be creative in designing new programs.

Inviting Leaders and Members to
Seek God's Will Rather than Their Own

One of the biggest impediments to creating a congregation of mystics has to do with how we decide issues within most mainline churches and denominations. *Robert's Rules of Order* has been a tremendous blessing to the life of most congregations and denominations, but with *Robert's Rules* has come spiritual dilemma. While they have brought order to the pandemonium that used to characterize church meetings prior to the 19th century, they simultaneously diminish God's role in decision-making. These guidelines have pushed God to the margins precisely by ensuring a fair democratic process in which the majority rules. Is majority rule the same as God's rule?

There is nothing in scripture that suggests that God's will is inherently found in the majority. What scripture does say is that the will of Christ is to be our aim. Unfortunately, our system of bringing forth issues for discussion, debate, and vote emphasizes the will of the people rather than the will of Christ.

An alternative way of leading a church supplements *Robert's Rules* by emphasizing discernment and seeking God's will over our own. As Charles Olsen and Danny Morris have demonstrated in their book *Discerning God's Will*, there is another way that entails framing issues in terms of what Christ is calling us to do.[4] It encourages leaders and church boards to discuss issues, ask questions, and then prayerfully seek God's will for the church. In voting on an issue, it entails asking the board to vote on what they sense God's will is for the church. Simply by leading a vote with, "All who sense this may be God's will say yes," rather than "All in favor say yes" (which is a vote based on the majority, not God) dramatically changes the church because it emphasizes the pursuit and discernment of God's will rather than our own.

From Reactive to Proactive to Spirit-Active Ministry

Throughout my ministry I have read many books and attended many conferences with a compelling message: We need to move from reactive to proactive ministry. I believe this wholeheartedly. Too many churches spin their wheels trying to react to the whirlwind of life around them. It's much better to be proactive, to gain a sense of what is coming, to plan ahead, and be prepared. The problem with proactivity is that it is rooted in rational analysis and careful planning based on reasonable future projections. What's so bad about that? Who can complain about leaders who analyze a church's needs and cautiously plan for the future? The problem is that it is leadership rooted in human analysis and planning rather than in discernment, faith, and service.

When rationally analyzing needs and problems becomes more important than discerning God's will, God gets left out of the decision making. When careful planning becomes more important than faith and service, people end up relying on their own judgment rather than on seeking God's will. They become more interested in following "the faith" rather than in following God "in faith."

Claude King tells a wonderful story demonstrating how human analysis and planning can actually inhibit God's work.[5] In 1984, King set out to make his mark in the world by serving God. A recent seminary graduate, he felt called to be a tent-making pastor planting new churches. He read every book he could on church planting, analyzed likely areas to plant churches, and made careful plans for building a congregation. He spent 18 months putting together his "business" plan. Then nothing happened. For six years he waited for a chance to start a church and put his plans into action, but all he encountered were obstacles and disinterest from others.

Then he met Henry Blackaby, a popular teacher in the area of faith and service. Blackaby taught him that we can't serve God unless we are first rooted in prayer and faith. Ministry needs to be a faithful response to God's calling, not activity based on our own plans for God. So King rooted his plans in prayer. He joined a local organization devoted to grounding church plantings in prayer. An amazing thing happened. They visited local churches and asked people to join them in prayerfully seeking God's will. After just three months, they had a list of fourteen towns or groups that wanted to start churches. They had become "Spirit-active" rather than merely reactive or proactive.

To be Spirit-active means to act on a foundation of prayer in a way that trusts the Holy Spirit to work through us. A mystical congregation understands this. No matter what ministries they attempt, they resist the temptation to program for program's sake. They don't look at the needs around them and say, "Let's start a program to deal with this need." They see the world around them and ask, "God, how are you calling us to respond?" They then let the Spirit guide them to develop and form unique ministries.

Being Spirit-active means growing organically as a church, responding to opportunities as the Spirit presents them to us. This is a much easier way of doing ministry because it means doing things when the time is ripe. It doesn't force ministry or mission, but lets it grow according to God's timetable. It is a way of doing ministry and leading a church that is much more relaxed because it resists the temptation to do for doing's sake that afflicts so many churches.

Openness to Mystical Experience

Some members, and especially leaders, of many churches distrust and fear mystical experiences. As a result, they are skeptical of people who have numinous experiences—experiences of God that transcend normal human experience—such as discernments, visions, near death experiences, or supernatural events. Often, when people share their experiences among church members, they are treated as though they are a bit weird, and their experiences are dismissed as being "just their imagination." What's ironic is that most sermons are based on either the mystical experiences of biblical figures or spiritual teachings on how we can encounter and experience God.

The truth is that many church members have had mystical experiences, and it is a mystical experience of God's call that led most pastors to become pastors. Encouraging members and leaders to share their mystical experiences opens the church spiritually by making spiritual seeking and experience the norm rather than the exception. For instance, last year our church published a small booklet as a Lenten resource called "Calvin Stories" that contained self-written stories by members of the church about their mystical experiences of God. As pastor, I also tell stories in my sermons of mystical experiences, both my own and those of others (with permission) in order to help people recognize that it is normal for Christians to have these experiences.

Becoming a mystical congregation means becoming a place where mystical experiences are both accepted and expected. To nurture this kind of acceptance, leaders have to create a culture and ethos of church in which stories of God experiences are valued and shared by encouraging pastoral and lay leaders, who share their own experiences of God through sermons, newsletters, Web sites, groups, and conversations. Ultimately, creating a congregation of mystics means creating a culture of mystical experience.

To Become a Congregation of Mystics

The path to becoming a congregation of mystics is not necessarily an easy path because it requires that we overcome resistance from members and leaders who are skeptical of the mystical. How do we make this transition? It all begins in prayer by asking God to lead us.

Leaders also must become gentle guides, recognizing that this path is a scary one for people who are used to believing that God is distant. This kind of transformation takes years of gentle guidance that continually calls people deeper into the mystical life.

Finally, we leaders have to be sure that in creating a congregation of mystics we don't try to create God or the church in our own image. We must look for opportunities to move the church in God's direction, even when it is different from our direction. Ultimately, to be a congregation of mystics means to be a congregation that grows in Christ to become Christ's body in our own unique places.

Notes

1. *Hungryhearts,* Winter 2004, Vol. XIII, No. 4 (Louisville, Ky.: Office of Spiritual Formation of the Presbyterian Church (USA)).
2. Thomas Kelly, *A Testament of Devotion* (San Francisco: HarperCollins, 1992), 54.
3. N. Graham Standish, *Becoming a Blessed Church: Forming a Church of Spiritual Purpose, Presence, and Power* (Herndon, Va.: Alban Institute, 2005).
4. Danny E. Morris and Charles M. Olsen, *Discerning God's Will Together: A Spiritual Practice for the Church* (Herndon, Va.: Alban Institute, 1997).
5. Henry Blackaby and Claude King, *Experiencing God: How to Live the Full Adventure of Knowing and Doing the Will of God* (Nashville: Broadman and Holman Publishers, 1994), x–xii.

Leading for the Future

JEFFREY D. JONES

In the past, pastoral leadership was all about playing various roles: preacher, teacher, counselor, administrator, social activist and more. In the future those roles will no longer describe the effective pastor. We already see signs of it. Pastors schooled in all the right roles and skilled at playing them still find themselves presiding over declining churches, buffeted by complaining parishioners, and wondering why their answers don't work anymore.

The roles worked well in a time of stability and continuity. Pastors equipped to play a limited number of clearly defined roles could count on providing effective ministry for their congregations. But in a time of rapid and tectonic change, just playing the roles doesn't do the job any more. And in the future, as change becomes even more profound, its impact compounds, and its pace increases, the roles will become even less meaningful. They won't work because they will no longer accomplish the work that must be done.

Leading for the future isn't a matter of roles or even the development of new roles. The diversity of ministry settings created by the change that is now taking place will make it impossible to define a set of roles that will ensure effective ministry for pastors. Even if it were possible, these roles would become outmoded and ineffective as rapidly as they were defined. In the future it won't be about roles. What will matter most is qualities. Leadership effectiveness will be shaped not be playing the right roles but by embodying the right qualities.

Originally published in *Congregations*, vol. 32, no. 1 (Winter 2006), pp. 14–17.

So, what are the qualities that will be most significant in a time of rapid and profound change, when old answers don't work and new ones have yet to be discovered? What are the qualities that are essential for leadership in a time of instability and uncertainty and yet filled with potential for new and deeper faithfulness?

It's perhaps best not to develop a checklist of qualities. That's a bit too mechanistic, too rigid for the uncertainty we face. Instead, let's play with some metaphors of possibility.

Leaders for the future have the heart of a servant. To be a servant leader means to understand that our purpose is to live for others. This isn't a matter of attending to others' every expressed need or fulfilling whatever demands they might have. True servanthood is something radically different; it is based in the belief that fulfillment comes as we discover God's intentions for us and bring them to reality in our lives. The servant, then, is one who works to make that possible. This will need to be the primary focus of the relationships and ministry of leaders for the future. This means that we enter into any leadership position with great humility. We are not there to have our own needs met. Some lead because it feels good to exercise power. Others lead because it feels good to help others. Both miss the point of servant leadership.

To be a servant is to empty one's self so that motivations are not based in personal ego satisfaction but in the potential growth of others. Let's be clear: This *is not* about becoming a doormat, of being so self-deprecating and self-sacrificing that we do injury to ourselves and our own well-being. That would be to deny the person God created us to be. Sometimes sacrifice is needed, but it always comes from our strength, not our weakness—from our ability to say yes, not our inability to say no. The importance of having the heart of a servant is not a new idea. Jesus himself talked about it. In the future, this kind of heart will need to be constantly beating in the life and work of the leader.

Leaders for the future have the mind of an architect. They will be about creating functional beauty. The newness of the future calls for an act of creation. What we create must be a thing of beauty that embodies the richness of God's kingdom in our time and place. The great challenge of the architect is to be both an artist and a mechanic—to see the grand design and at the same time attend to the details, to create a thing of beauty that works effectively. In the same way, leaders for the future will need to "think big" in order to envision the wonder of a new way of being church, of encountering the holy, of participating in God's mission. This great creation will need to be a thing a beauty so that it expresses the beauty of God's love for the world and attracts those whose lives are so often drab and dreary. And yet at the same time it will need to function effectively. This functionality is what makes the beauty of the creation a reality in the lives of people, applying it to their lives in specific ways that respond to their needs. In order to be both beautiful and functional, the "building" will need to have a solid biblical and theological foundation and its "mechanical systems" will need to respond to those who occupy it. It might be a tabernacle or a temple, but whatever it is, it must have a functional beauty. Creating that takes the mind of an architect.

Leaders for the future have the spirit of an ascetic. The desert mothers and fathers of the fourth century understood what it took to remain faithful in a world that was suddenly different. Their genius was in going deeper into the self in order to know God more deeply. This self-knowledge is essential for faithful leaders. It is what enables the personal transformation that makes transformative leadership possible. It is what rids us of (or at least makes us aware of) all the failings and foibles, the sins and self-centeredness that keep us from living for others. It is what gives us the humility to know that the challenge we face is one we are not equal to on our own. It is what helps us recognize our complete and total dependence on God in order to be the leaders that will help form a future according to God's vision. And, beyond ourselves, our awareness of this dependence is what attunes us to the work of God in the lives of others and in the world. This is what enables us to see God where others don't, to name God's presence, and to align ourselves with God's mission. It is this spirit that leads us to reaffirm, even in the midst of our secular world, that God is at work and that the world truly is in God's hands.

Leaders for the future have the arms of a hugger. The desert fathers and mothers, as isolated as they seemed to be, knew that community was essential to their faith and well-being. They spent hours alone delving the depths of their beings, but they also came together to share and to worship. Community has always been a part of congregational life, but the community of the future will be different, more difficult to develop, and because of that probably more authentic. It won't be a community based on similarity of race, culture, economic status, or theology. It will be a community of genuine diversity, not just because diversity is valued (which, of course, it should be) but because diversity will be unavoidable. Even though the urge to retreat to cultural, racial, economic, and theological enclaves may be great, God is already at work in the world to deny such narrowness. Everywhere we turn we are confronted with those who are different from us in countless ways. In the future there will be no escape from diversity, so leadership in the future will need to evidence a warm inclusivity. The arms of a hugger reach out to gather in all who would come, to welcome them, to embrace them, to bring them together into a new creation—a beloved community.

Leaders for the future have the strength of a gymnast. Gymnasts amaze me. It's not just their physical strength—which allows them to balance on beams and suspend themselves on rings—that I marvel at. It is also their strength of spirit, which allows them to focus and perform these near miraculous feats under great pressure and in the midst of great distractions. Imagine the fortitude it takes to run full speed into failure. That's essentially what a gymnast does on every vault. The chances of achieving the perfect 10 on a vault are infinitesimal. The chances of missing the landing are great, even for accomplished gymnasts. And yet they are able to focus their effort, marshal their strength of both body and spirit, and enter into the challenge ahead of them. And they are able to bounce back quickly from a failure in order to try again, perhaps taking an even greater risk this time. That's the kind of strength leaders for the future need. It will need to be a strength that enables us to focus even in the face of possible (and maybe even likely) failure, because the answers do not exist and even the clues are not clear. It will need to be a strength that allows us to move into the challenge ahead of us with great intensity (if not necessarily great speed), even if we cannot be sure of the outcome, because anything less will lack the energy needed for the task at hand.

Leaders for the future have the legs of a marathoner. Marathoners are in it for the long haul, and so must be leaders for the future. The work that needs to be done won't be accomplished soon. The transitions that are taking place in society are leading us to something new, but we don't yet know what that is and probably won't know for some time to come. It is, after all, a postmodern, post-Christendom world we live in now. We are unable to describe it in any way other than to say what it is not. Someday we will know what it is, but we've got a way to go until then. That means leaders for the future will need to stick with their mission. They will need to try and fail and try again. They will need to keep learning, discovering, discerning the new things God is doing and calling us to become. They will need to deal with those who resist change, those who clamor for more and faster change, those who are tired, those who are fearful, those who are annoyed, those who want to give up.

Perhaps the most striking physical characteristic of the marathoner is leanness. That's also a trait of leaders for the future. They must be lean, free of the baggage of the past, having set aside the programs and priorities that no longer serve their purpose. The journey into the future cannot be successful with a lot of baggage. Leanness is essential for the long haul.

Leaders for the future have the soul of a poet. Poets help us see in new ways. They combine words and images in ways that create new realities for us. They help us feel, as well as think. Pain is expressed rather than internalized. Hope emerges from despair. Impossibility becomes reality.

Leaders for the future are poets. They help us see what we could not see before, creating new possibility, new reality, for us. They show us where God is at work, where God's justice is being made real, where God's kingdom is being formed. They help us understand that, ultimately, as uncertain, as insecure, as different as it may be, this future we are moving into is God's future. They help us have faith.

We've been playing with metaphors here, not creating a checklist. Even so, what has been described probably seems impossible. Embodying these qualities in one person approaches being a ridiculous fantasy. Don't worry about it! This leader for the future doesn't exist and never will. The leader for the future isn't a person. It is a team. It is a group of people gifted and called by God to lead. It is a community drawn together by a sense of the possible within a congregation and committed to make God's kingdom just a bit more real in their time and place. This fact alone changes the notions of leadership that pastors and congregations have operated under for years. It breaks down barriers between professional and lay leaders. It blurs the distinctions between clergy and laity. It refocuses our attention on gifts and call as being the basis for ministry.

When gifts and call become the basis for ministry, our whole understanding of "who does what" in the congregation changes. If gifts and call are the basis for ministry, the assumed distinctions between clergy and laity disappear. What matters most is not title or role but the gifts that have been given and the call that has been answered. This focus on gifts and call also leads us to a new humility about leadership. It reminds us that no one has all the gifts, but all the gifts are present within the Body. That is why a leadership team is essential for the future. When the challenges before us are great we need to take advantage of every gift God has given. That is only possible if we approach the task of leadership as a team.

This leads us to one final affirmation about leaders for the future. Many of the qualities we've already discussed are important to team-building. Someone in each congregation, however, will need to see his or her primary call as bringing together the group that embodies these qualities, as well as others that the congregation might need. That responsibility requires the eyes of Jesus to see the gifts in others and call them into ministry. The team may include clergy and laity, paid staff and volunteers. The team leader's responsibility will be to gather those who are needed, guide the development of a common vision for their work, and support and encourage their efforts. Often the pastor will be expected to play this role. That may very well be the way to do it, but it doesn't have to be. Remember, it is the gifts that matter most, the gifts that determine the responsibilities we take on. However, the pastor, at the very least, will need to understand this and encourage it, whether he or she is the team leader or not.

This team will serve two essential roles in the life of the congregation. First, it will provide the leadership that is needed, guiding the congregation as a whole into the future to which God is calling it. Second, and just as important, it will model a way of working for others in the congregation. If it is a community that embodies the reality of spirit-directed leadership based in gifts, it will provide the example for others to follow as they begin to discern their gifts and call and move into God's mission. The leadership team will provide the model for the ministry teams that will be essential to congregations of the future.

The focus for our playful encounter with these metaphors of possibility has been leadership *for* the future, not leadership *in* the future or *of* the future. If we wait for the future, we'll be too late. Right now is the time to begin to let go of roles and embrace qualities. Right now is the time to begin to develop the gifts and discern the call of those who will be part of the leader team. The future is already in our midst. Leadership for the future begins today.

Leading Theologically: Does It Really Matter?

R. SCOTT COLGLAZIER

Juxtaposing two of the most significant religion stories of the summer of 2003 might seem as odd as combining peanut butter and tuna fish. What common element links the election of a gay bishop in the Episcopal Church and a controversial movie about the crucifixion of Jesus produced by Hollywood star Mel Gibson? Despite the odd pairing, I think these two stories reveal a third story—the presence of a deep fissure running through the landscape of American Christianity, one that is testing and reshaping the nature of Christian faith, and therefore creating a leadership challenge to ministers in congregational settings. Precisely because of this challenge, churches are desperate not only for leadership, but particularly for theological leadership from clergy.

Cultural Lightning Rod

In the case of Bishop V. Gene Robinson, who was consecrated November 2, 2003, in the Episcopal Diocese of New Hampshire, his story has become a cultural lightning rod for the complex issue of homosexuality and the church. What one thinks about the particulars of this issue is not within the purview of this article. My concern is that the issue itself is an example of why the church needs theological leadership at the congregational level.

Originally published in *Congregations,* vol. 30, no. 1 (Winter 2004), pp. 10–13.

Armed with a literal reading of the Bible, some Christians declare, often with acrimonious enthusiasm, that homosexuality is a sin and that homosexuals are condemned by God. Behind this interpretation lies the belief that the Bible is the literal word of God and that it has come to the world without error. Others believe that the Bible is condemning exploitive behavior—not a particular sexual orientation, but behavior that is abusive and aggressive. In the centuries and cultures in which the Bible was written, people couldn't have comprehended a person's "being" homosexual in any psychological or physiological sense. In addition, if the gospel of Christ is about God's gracious welcome, then the church should be welcoming to all people—including people of different sexual orientations.

Not surprisingly, Christians on opposite sides of the issue often find themselves sitting side by side in the congregation and listening to the same sermon on Sunday morning. The first group understands God's will as an ancient standard that must be followed strictly, while others argue that God is "in process" with the church, inspiring compassion and understanding for an evolving human situation. This issue, like many others, swirls about in local churches, as well as outside organized religion. Sadly, complex theological issues often receive only superficial treatment on the six o'clock news. The focus is often on titillating controversy rather than on theological complexity. This kind of media superficiality, however, opens an opportunity for ministers as they work with congregations. The challenge is to help churches become learning communities where theological ideas can be explored in serious and respectful ways.

An Outcry over a Film

The same dynamics are at play in relation to Mel Gibson's much disputed film on the crucifixion of Jesus. Gibson, a fundamentalist Catholic, has made a film that slavishly (and graphically) follows the biblical accounts of the crucifixion of Jesus. The film clearly has created an enormous theological stir within both print and electronic media because it opens an ancient theological wound in portraying the Jews as killers of the Son of God.

Gibson seems oblivious to the fact that biblical "accounts" of the crucifixion are quite unlike the reasonably accurate, contemporary blow-by-blow journalistic reports or "accounts" of a trial and execution. Often the Gospel writers differ in their recounting of details about the death of Jesus. They also emphasize differing theological motifs within their Passion narratives. For the most part, the Gospel writers were more concerned with what was happening at the end of the first century of the Christian era in their own churches than with what happened on the day Jesus was crucified. This is not to suggest that the biblical accounts of crucifixion are without historical reliability. In my estimation, that would overstate the case. At the same time, it's fair to say that the Gospels are more theological documents than strict histories.

Throughout the summer, Gibson insisted that he was trying to make a movie true to the biblical accounts of the crucifixion, but what he apparently wound up doing was proliferating one of the most haunting falsehoods in Christian history—namely, the notion that the Jews killed Jesus. The church is still trying to come to terms with the damage this dimension of Christian theology has done to the world. Making villains of the Jews, primarily in the Gospel of John, reflects a strained relationship between the church and the synagogue at the end of the first century, and not a strict reflection of historical fact surrounding the death of Jesus.

Developing Communities of Growth

Mel Gibson's movie, which received wide discussion in the national media, offers another theological opportunity for clergy to exhibit leadership within their congregations. How one feels about the issue or what position one finally takes is not nearly as important as congregations addressing such matters in honest and engaging ways. How can the church become a place where issues such as anti-Judaism are understood from a theological perspective? How can communities of faith grow into communities of dialogue, moving past old labels of "liberal" and "conservative" to become settings where people learn together?

Important theological dialogue can take place within local churches, but rarely does it happen without well-thought-out leadership from clergy. These two major news stories from summer 2003 suggest that two kinds of churches are slowly developing in American culture—"answer" churches and "journey" churches.[1] *Answer* churches find their beliefs neatly packaged in the Bible; therefore their approach becomes adherence to well-defined beliefs, *Journey* churches, on the other hand, understand faith as an ongoing discovery. They understand that listening to the Bible is a process (yes, the Bible is taken seriously in journey churches); but in addition to heeding the Bible, journey churches listen for God's voice in the continuing development of culture.

A Polarized Church

I'm not sure the Christian landscape has ever been more polarized than it is now, and I don't anticipate its becoming less divided in the future. Yet because the landscape is, at base, a theological one, clergy have an opportunity to initiate responsible religious dialogue within their churches. Sometimes theological issues emerge from the church itself; at other times, issues are thrust upon the church by a media blitz. Either way, the opportunity for lively, meaningful, and respectful theological conversation will present itself.

Theological leadership can be exhibited in a variety of ways. First and foremost, theological leadership is manifested not so much by anything the minister *does,* but by virtue of who he or she is. When a minister thinks theologically and follows the larger arcs of meaning that have always been a part of religious life, the congregation soon picks up on this approach and realizes that the pastor has a certain spiritual and intellectual fire burning inside his or her being. It has a luminous quality. Whether the minister is standing in the pulpit, officiating at a wedding, or engaged in casual conversation in the parking lot, the glow of theological energy is present.

To use an analogy, some chefs work in the kitchen because it is their job. Other chefs, however, are always thinking creatively about food. They talk to their customers about it and seek out conversations with other chefs and even travel to learn more. When you are around this kind of chef, it takes about five minutes to discover that food is much more than a job; it's a passion.

Theological Reflection as Passion

In much the same way, congregations notice if theological reflection is part of their pastor's passion, if it's an ongoing experience for the minister and not something that was finished back in seminary. When the minister continues to explore theologically—always curious, always pushing, probing, and reading—the congregation begins to see a fresh faith that matters to our world today. The minister is then viewed by the congregation not merely as a pastor or administrator, but as an interpreter of the Christian faith amid the people of God.

When theological reflection comes from the essential center of a minister, it radiates through the act of preaching. There is, to be sure, a place for the courageous, prophetic sermon, but the best preaching creates an invitation for the listener to think and feel, to consider how God and world are intersecting in any given issue. The invitation is not "Listen to me because I have all the answers." Rather, it is more like "Join me on the journey as I try to understand my faith in light of what is happening in my church and world." Even when the issue is as complex as homosexuality, the minister can speak about it in a way that gives people room to struggle and grow. Edges of such theological issues have to be pushed. At the same time, the theological conclusion finally reached is not nearly so important as the theological process that has been engaged.

Beyond Preaching

The issues of homosexuality and a movie about Jesus's crucifixion give rise to all kinds of religious questions: What is the nature of the Bible? In what way is the Bible authoritative in the life of the church? How do we understand modern psychology in light of ancient concepts about humanity? What claim does the spirit of Jesus have on the church community, particularly in relation to the acceptance of others? Not only can preaching become a model of theological exploration, it can inspire dialogue by addressing the real issues simmering in our culture.

But beyond preaching, ministers can foster theological dialogue and transformation in other ways. Perhaps a few examples from

my experience at University Christian Church in Fort Worth will
illustrate:

- We have created a dialogue for Jewish, Christian, and Islamic
  faiths. This project is not only good for our own church; it
  also sends out signals to the larger Fort Worth community
  that our congregation is a place where faith is taken seriously
  and inclusively.

- A few years ago, recognizing that our church's elders basically
  spent their meetings talking about business items nonstop, we
  created elder dialogue sessions devoted to nothing but a
  particular theological topic. In recent years, we have explored
  such topics as prayer, Christology, and the nature of religious
  authority. Interestingly enough, the elders of the church had
  been bored with their business sessions for years and were
  glad to have a chance to learn about their faith. This year we
  are using an excellent book titled *How to Think Theologically.*[2]
  The goal of these sessions is not to reach total agreement on a
  theological topic; it is to help these lay leaders become more
  theologically aware.

- We have created continuing programs of theological
  reflection around film, literature, and art, allowing us to
  explore intersections of faith and culture. We have read books
  by Elie Wiesel, Chaim Potok, Anne Lamott, and James Carroll,
  to name a few. We have explored such movies as *Life is
  Beautiful* and *As Good As It Gets* to understand faith and
  redemption. We also have regular outings to museums to
  discover religious themes in art.

- We have sponsored travel experiences ranging from a
  women's visit to the border areas of Mexico and Texas to
  study the plight of immigrant families, to intergenerational
  study trips to Italy, where families explored some of the great
  Christian art traditions in Florence and Rome. Even our
  service-type trips lend themselves to theological reflection.

- We have also created successful theological dialogue by using
  our small-group ministry of ChristCare. These small groups

always study the sermon text that I will use on Sunday morning. This practice creates a dialogue—not only with the biblical text but also with the larger worship life of the church. Moreover, it creates a theological dialogue between laypeople and senior minister. Our church is greatly enhanced by the fact that people show up on Sunday already in conversation with the theme of the morning.

Teaching People to Outgrow Anti-Judaism

There are always theological needs within the church, and therefore, always opportunities for reflection in the life of Christians. Perhaps this is my own bias, but given that so much of today's religious landscape is shaped by a more literal, fundamentalist approach to religion, mainline Protestants have a special challenge to create an alternative religious discourse, not only for their churches but also for the culture at large.

A pastor can do something as simple as leading the congregation in a study of anti-Judaism. One immensely interesting possibility would be a Lenten Bible study experience focusing on the Passion narratives, leading people through an exploration of how the Bible emerged in the life of the church. This study would offer a way of talking about the church's witness to the gospel and how that witness can be made without any implicit or explicit anti-Jewish thought. It would also serve as a reflection on the liturgy of the church during Lent and Holy Week.

People can be helped to understand how a certain strand of Christian witness has been intrinsically anti-Jewish (including some of the witness found in the Bible), and how damaging such a witness has been to the Jewish people. They can also learn to appreciate the need for the church to think theologically while taking into account the implications of the Holocaust. And finally, the church has a way to think critically about a contemporary movie on the death of Jesus—a film that at one level might seem completely harmless, but at a deeper level may well betray the fundamental beauty of the Christian witness.

Answer Churches, Journey Churches

Our culture will always have "answer" churches—those communities of faith that tend to see a well-defined Christianity. But for other churches, "journey" churches, theological exploration is essential because these churches thrive not by suggesting, "It doesn't matter what you believe," but by inviting people into the adventure of theological reflection and discovery, which in the end is a process of discovering what it means to be a human being in this world.

In my experience, people in churches are hungry for theological leadership, for the opportunity to grapple with everything from a news story about a controversial Episcopal bishop to an eyebrow-raising contemporary movie about Jesus. Clergy leadership should be measured not merely by how well the church is administered or how many new members are received or how many pastoral calls are completed. All of that is important, but if there is such a thing as a "calling" (a profoundly religious concept), then clergy leaders should be about the business of creating religious community—one of theological exploration and discourse. Such communities rarely form by accident. They emerge when pastors are willing to lead theologically—leading because they passionately believe that it matters.

Notes

1. R. Scott Colglazier, *A Larger Hope: Opening the Heart to God* (St. Louis: Chalice Press, 2002).
2. Howard Stone and James Duke, *How to Think Theologically* (Minneapolis: Fortress Press, 1996).

Lift High the Flag ... Oops, the Cross!

DIANA BUTLER BASS

A week after the September 11 terrorist attacks, I had lunch with some of my students at Virginia Theological Seminary in Alexandria. As part of their program, first-year students are required to visit churches in the area. Over lunch that day, they were discussing what they had witnessed in northern Virginia congregations on the Sunday after the attacks.

"At the church I visited, the congregation sang 'America the Beautiful' as a prayer on their knees," one student reported.

"We sang nothing but patriotic songs," another remarked, "It was disturbing. There was no mention of Christ."

"The flag came in the procession before the cross," another groaned.

"That's nothing," one young man said. "At the church I visited the priest carried in the flag, put it next to the altar and announced that it would stay there 'until this whole thing is over.' Then he said, 'If you don't like it, you are in the wrong church.'"

I listened with sympathetic interest to their observations and anxieties about the mixture of church and nationalism that surfaced in the wake of the September 11 horrors. I, too, had stories. As a member of the senior staff at Christ Church, a large Episcopal parish in Alexandria that is five miles from the Pentagon, I knew what it was like on the inside. Within hours of the attacks, well-meaning parishioners had called the church requesting that Sunday worship be changed to include such

---

Originally published in *Congregations*, vol. 28, no. 1 (January/February 2002), pp. 24–28.

elements as a full military color guard, the singing of the national anthem, the playing of taps, and patriotic bunting draped about the church.

While the senior staff agreed that it was theologically and spiritually inappropriate to turn Sunday Eucharist into a patriotic requiem, we found it difficult to resist the tide of nationalism—and even militarism—rolling through our congregation. After much soul-searching, we compromised and chose "My Country, 'Tis Of Thee" to be sung at the offertory. And the flag was carried in as part of the procession. However, even that nod toward patriotic fervor disturbed me. September 11 did not cause me to flee to the flag; I found myself on my knees before the cross. I could not understand what the church members wanted—or why they wanted it. When I heard my students' reports, I at least understood that I was not alone with my fears that the church was wrapping the suffering and bleeding Christ in a flag.

Whatever personal comfort I found around the refectory table that day, many disturbing theological and pastoral questions remained. How was I, as a leader in a congregation, to address questions of faith and nation, of church and state, of reconciliation and military action? How to be both pastoral and prophetic? Was I called to be both comforter and transformer at the same time? What is the role of congregational leadership during terrorism and war? The task was overwhelming—I had never felt more inadequate in ministry. September 11 was calling me to be a better leader, to maintain theological clarity, and to rise to the spiritual challenge ahead.

Know Where You Stand

The first aspect of effective leadership in a crisis is understanding where you, as a leader, stand theologically amid the questions. The priest who planted the flag next to the altar knew his mind on these issues. I may think he is wrong, but it is clear what he thinks.

Many midlife and younger churchgoers and leaders have spent little time thinking about their theologies of Christ and culture. It has been 30 or 40 years since many congregations and denominations have seriously addressed issues of church and state. When I was a girl growing up in a Methodist church, the conflict between flag and cross created intense debates as we grappled with both the civil rights movement and the Vietnam war. As a baby boomer, as a leader in my congregation and my denomination, I have found that those debates were formative in my theology and my spiritual life.

Today's religious leaders—a host of people like me—were children or teenagers during the last major historical point of crisis over faith and nationalism. The answers—or nonanswers—to questions of church and state drove many of us away from traditional churches. Or at least, the issues and arguments caused us to wonder about the relevance of religious belief in the public arena. Could the gospel reconcile racial divisions? Did the Christian story truly proclaim peace? Was the institutional church committed to Jesus's message of transformation?

Because of the church's inability to lead during a time of cultural crisis and violence, I suspect that many of today's lay leaders and clergy feel ambivalent or angry about the current outburst of religious nationalism. For weeks, I felt a deep hostility toward my congregation and at odds with the conflation of flag and faith that I witnessed. At times, I wondered if I was suffering theological insanity as I realized how much my feelings and ideals diverged from those of others. My confusion drove me back to theological reflection—asking myself what I believed about the relationship between Christ and culture, what the Bible says, and what my life experience has taught me. As I thought, prayed, and studied, my sense of call and vocation became clearer.

Although I am an Episcopalian, I am deeply influenced by the Lutheran doctrine of two kingdoms and the profoundly paradoxical relationship between God's reign and earthly political states. I confess that a "wannabe" Quaker lurks within the recesses of my soul. After rereading Reinhold Niebuhr's *Christ and Culture*, bits of Augustine's *City of God*, the Gospel of Luke, and the book of Romans, I found myself spiritually steadied and "in line" with historic Christian tradition. Knowing my heart and theological passions helped me over the feelings of anger, ambivalence, and doubt. This confidence enabled me to see better what I might teach and preach to those whom I am called to serve. My views, feelings, and beliefs were not wrong—they were simply different from those held by the most vocal segment of the congregation. And I needed to recognize that, because of years of theological training and reflection, I as a leader had something to say and teach at a time of crisis that could serve as a loving corrective to some of the misunderstandings of flag and cross.

Knowing I was not crazy helped. But being reminded that I am a Lutheran-Quaker-Episcopalian did not solve all my ministry problems. The second aspect of effective leadership is to understand where your tradition stands. In this sense, "tradition" means both the grand narrative of the denomination and its local expression in a particular congregation.

Some denominations have better theological resources than others to sort out issues of faith and the flag. Baptists, Lutherans, Roman Catholics, and Anabaptists have well-developed and clear theologies of church and state. For those groups, September 11 provided an opportunity to return to tradition and to understand fundamental aspects of denominational or congregational identity.

But much of American religion—especially Presbyterianism, Congregationalism, and Methodism—is not so clear about religious nationalism. Part of my anxiety arose from the realization that I belong to a denomination that has no unified theology of church and state. The Episcopal Church in the United States speaks with two conflicting voices: one declaring that the church should never address any political concern from its pulpits; the other contending that the church serves as a kind of national temple where people of all faiths can pray with dignity and decorum.

Thus, my denomination vacillates between complete avoidance and total embrace of nationalist piety. On any given day, the Episcopal Church might eschew addressing justice issues as inappropriate; or it might surrender a major pulpit to the president of the United States. Although this inconsistency might seem an incomprehensible theological mishmash to others, it makes a modicum of sense to Episcopalians. Our tradition is that of comprehension, the church of irreconcilable opposites, both Protestant and Catholic. Contradictions are part of our identity—the church of the *via media*. Part of our strength is our willingness to live with our dizzying diversity

In my parish, however, the grand denominational narrative of the "middle way" has often given way to one side of the debate. Founded in 1767, Christ Church was the home parish of George Washington and, later, of Robert E. Lee. For most of its history, it has functioned as a faithful congregation worshiping in a chapel of American civil religion. As long as "faithful congregation" and "American civil religion" did not conflict, things went along swimmingly—that is, up until the 1960s and 1970s. At that point, Christ Church began to lose members—as did thousands of other mainline congregations—when the flag seemed at odds with racial justice and international peace.

Christ Church waved the American flag against civil rights and con-scientious objection to war. Historically, we have a miserable record of race relations. In one infamous incident during the Vietnam war, an Alexandria judge, who also served as senior warden of the vestry (gov-erning board) at Christ Church, threw the book at some Episcopal semi-narians arrested for conducting a "peace Eucharist" and blocking an entrance to the Pentagon. Members of the younger generation left in droves. The only congregants who stayed around were their World War II parents and grandparents, many of whom were war veterans, whose theological perspectives and life experience kept faith and flag together in a way reminiscent of the 1950s.

When baby boomers started returning to church in the 1980s and 1990s, they generally turned a blind eye to our forebears George and "Bobby" (as the boomers and genXers irreverently call them), whose memorial plaques and portraits grace our walls. They also ignored the flag-waving of the senior generation. In short, the congregation had a polite generational cease-fire regarding church and state during the last two decades of the 20th century. After September 11, 2001, however, polite silence became difficult to maintain. And both sides of the gen-erational divide struggle to understand what has happened in a way that is consonant with their life experience.

Thus, the local expression of my tradition is one of civil religion, a tradition ignored, rejected, or scorned by the largest and most rapidly growing segment of the congregation—but a tradition still celebrated by the building's architecture and tourist brochures. In short, the congregation's church-and-state tradition is changing (and has changed), and congregants are confused, hurt, and at a theological loss to know where to turn. The only people with clarity are the "flag and faith" members—or the few Lutheran-Quaker-Episcopalians like me.

Some of the congregation wanted to sing the national anthem. After all, one of our celebrated 18th century parishioners—Francis Scott Key—wrote it! The tide of American history, profoundly confusing the New Israel and the United States, is our history too.

But it is not our only history. Our congregation's history is also that of the returning baby boomers and generation X members who fill our pews. Their theological story—the way in which they respond to this crisis—will become part of local tradition and the larger story of our denomination. The faithfulness of the September 11 generation will be knit into the 225-year history of a congregation—as was their parents' and grandparents' theological interpretation of America.

And that is where good leadership matters.

Why Leadership Matters

Why not simply wave the flag and sing "God Bless America"? After all, patriotism seems to be helping millions of Americans to hold on to sanity and summon courage. Why not enlist the church in this moral defense of the homeland?

The issue for American congregations is confusion. As some thoughtful Christians—including C.S. Lewis and G.K. Chesterton—pointed out during the 20th century, patriotism elicits feelings akin to religious ecstasy. Love of country can easily be confused with love of God. This confusion leads to profoundly negative outcomes.

Patriotism in churches fuels religious nationalism. Patriotism is so emotionally powerful that it can marshal masses to any cause, whether noble or misguided. Although our side believes its cause to be blessed by God, every side in every conflict and war has always believed that to be the case. When conflated with faith, patriotism becomes religious nationalism—a danger to both the secular state and the church. During the American Civil War, Abraham Lincoln plumbed the painful paradoxes of religious nationalism in his Second Inaugural Address: "Both [North and South] read the same Bible and pray to the same God; and each invokes His aid against the other. . . . The prayers of both could not be answered; that of neither has been answered fully. The Almighty has His own purposes."

Some people may protest that the current conflict is different from the one about which President Lincoln wrote so eloquently—Christians and Muslims do not read the same book or pray to the same God. But most mainline Protestants reject theological exclusivity in favor of recognizing the commonalities of Christian, Islamic, and Jewish monotheism and have expressed hopes for the universal reach of God's mysterious love. Religious nationalism is dangerous because it establishes American Christianity as normative by claiming (however subtly) that God is on our side.

Thus, patriotism enrolls the church as a soldier of the political order—the source of the very "evil" that President Bush decries. When the cross is draped with the flag, we become crusaders ourselves and give our enemies more reason to hate us. The echoes of Pope Urban II's call to destroy the infidel, "God wills it!" ring down through the ages to our own day. Unless we live into our best theological nature, the present conflict may teach us how little Christians have learned from history. Sadly enough, we could become a mirror image of what we seek to resist.

Patriotism, with its corresponding religious nationalism, also distracts from God's primary mission for the church: to love all peoples, to tear down walls of hatred and division, to reconcile those at war, and to serve the least among us. As an Episcopal bishop of Ohio, Charles P. McIlvaine, reminded his denomination in 1862, "Let not love of Country make your love to God . . . the less fervent. Immense as is this present earthly interest, it is only earthly. The infinitely greater interests of the soul and of the kingdom of God remain as paramount as ever."

It matters because, in the words of Bishop McIlvaine, "the soul and the kingdom of God" are at stake. Congregations are not chapels of the state or the military. They are outposts of God's mission. Our call at this moment is to serve grieving families, to give hope and courage to the fearful, and to pray, speak, and work for peace and its corresponding blessings of liberty and freedom. Our job is not to proclaim or seem to imply that our nation is blameless, morally pure, and God's righteous empire. In the wake of September 11, congregations must remember their fundamental vocation of healing souls and spreading God's reign of love.

What to Do

With the stakes so high, preaching and teaching take on new gravity. Congregations need to understand that this is not the time to "play church," as the senior minister at Christ Church said in his sermon September 16. Bunting, taps, and the national anthem are important—but they are not churchly. They are appropriate in the civic arena. Patriotism provides deeply meaningful, but theologically distracting, symbols. This is no time for theological confusion. The "infinitely greater interests" of soul and God's kingdom call our congregations to move beyond emotive symbols to faithful discipleship, peacemaking, and service to the poor, the outcast, and the oppressed.

As in the 1960s, what we do now will determine the faith we pass to our children and grandchildren. Will they see, believe, respond to God, and embrace a way of life that matters? Our response to terrorism and war tests our theological character, our spiritual integrity and our moral commitments. This is not only a battle for freedom; it is also an old-fashioned war for our souls. Winning may be important; how we win is even more so. The next generation is watching.

So is the world. The response of our congregations leavens American politics and policies. With patience, we may emerge from this time of troubles a wiser and more compassionate nation—something, I suspect, for which many of our brothers and sisters across the globe have long prayed. Chastened and strengthened by God's mercy and grace, we may help create a world where terrorism and violence no longer threaten the universal human hope to raise families, make decent and honorable livings, enjoy the world's beauties, worship and know God, and love our neighbors.

Contributors

Diana Butler Bass, is an independent scholar. From 2003–2006 she led the Project on Congregations of Intentional Practice. She is the author of *The Practicing Congregation: Imagining a New Old Church* (Alban, 2004) and *Christianity for the Rest of Us: How the Neighborhood Church Is Transforming the Faith* (HarperSanFrancisco, 2006).

Richard Bass is the director of publishing of the Alban Institute.

Mark Lau Branson is a Homer L. Goddard Associate Professor of the Ministry of the Laity at Fuller Theological Seminary in Pasadena, California, where he teaches courses in congregational leadership and community engagement. He is the author of *Memoris, Hopes, and Conversations: Appreciative Inquiry and Congregational Change* (Alban, 2004).

Christina Braudaway-Bauman serves as coordinator of the pastoral residency program at the Wellesley Congregational Church and as associate for new clergy development for the Massachusetts Conference, United Church of Christ (UCC).

R. Scott Colglazier, senior minister of University Christian Church in Fort Worth, Texas. He is currently interim chief program minister at Riverside Church in New York City. He is the author of *A Larger Hope: Opening the Heart to God* (Chalice, 2002).

Scott Eblin is president of the Eblin Group, a coaching and leadership development firm in Herndon, Virginia. He is the author of *The Next Level: What Insiders Know about Executive Success* (Davies-Black, 2006).

Howard Friend is the founder and lead consultant of the Parish Empowerment Network in West Chester, Pennsylvania. His books include *Recovering the Sacred Center: Church Renewal from the Inside Out* (Judson Press, 1998).

Art Gafke, at the time this article was written, was district superintendent of the Shasta District of the California-Nevada Annual Conference of the United Methodist Church.

Israel Galindo is a professor of Christian education at the Baptist Theological Seminary in Richmond, Virginia. He also serves as faculty for Leadership in Ministry Workshops (www.leadershipinministry.com), a clergy leadership training program, and is executive director of Educational Consultants, Inc. He is the author *The Hidden Lives of Congregations: Discerning Church Dynamics* (Alban, 2004).

Andrew D. Hagen, at the time this article was written, was mission pastor of a new congregation, Joyful Spirit, in Bolingbrook, Illinois. He is now senior pastor of Advent Lutheran Church in Boca Raton, Florida.

Bill Jones, at the time this article was written, was pastor of Balmoral Presbyterian Church in Memphis, Tennessee. He is now a professional storyteller.

Jeffrey D. Jones is the pastor of the First Baptist Church in Plymouth, Massachusetts. He also serves as director of distance learning at Andover Newton Theological School and is a member of the school's senior adjunct faculty. He is the author of *Traveling Together: A Guide for Disciple-Forming Congregations* (Alban, 2006).

Bruce McSpadden, at the time this article was written, was director of the San Francisco United Methodist Mission.

Gil Rendle is a senior consultant with the Alban Institute. His books include *Leading Change in the Congregation: Spiritual and Organizational Tools for Leaders* (Alban, 1998).

Donna Schaper, at the time this article was written, was senior pastor of Coral Gables Congregational Church in Coral Gables, Florida. She is now senior minister of Judson Memorial Church in New York City. She writes and speaks extensively and conducts creative writing workshops.

N. Graham Standish is pastor of Calvin Presbyterian Church in Zelienople, Pennsylvania. He is the author of *Becoming a Blessed Church: Forming a Church of Spiritual Purpose, Presence, and Power* (Alban, 2005). He is also an adjunct professor at Pittsburgh Theological Seminary, a retreat leader, and spiritual director.

Ann Svennungsen is president of the Fund for Theological Education. She served as a Lutheran pastor for 22 years, most recently as senior pastor of the 3,700-member Trinity Lutheran Church in Moorhead, Minnesota.

Edward A. White is a consultant with the Alban Institute. He is the author of *Saying Goodbye: A Time of Growth for Pastors and Congregations* (Alban, 1990).

Hollis R. Williams, Jr., at the time this article was written, was rector of Trinity Episcopal Church in Everett, Washington.

James P. Wind is the president of the Alban Institute.

David Wood is the coordinator of the Transition into Ministry program, funded by the Lilly Endowment.